I0796768

Spice It Up!

Fabulous flavor-packed recipes

pil

Publications International, Ltd.

Louis Weber, CEO
Publications International, Ltd.
8140 Lehigh Ave
Morton Grove, IL 60053

Pictured on the back cover *(clockwise from top left):* Cauliflower and Mushroom Tacos with Chipotle Crema *(page 154),* Hot Chicken Sandwiches *(page 180),* Jamaican Grilled Sweet Potatoes *(page 118),* Harissa Honey Chicken and Rice Bowls *(page 72),* Southwestern Chicken Chili *(page 50)* and Chipotle Lamb Chops with Crispy Potatoes *(page 166).*

ISBN: 978-1-63938-834-9

Manufactured in China.

8 7 6 5 4 3 2 1

Microwave Cooking: Microwave ovens vary in wattage. Use the cooking times as guidelines and check for doneness before adding more time.

WARNING: Food preparation, baking and cooking involve inherent dangers: misuse of electric products, sharp electric tools, boiling water, hot stoves, allergic reactions, foodborne illnesses and the like, pose numerous potential risks. Publications International, Ltd. (PIL) assumes no responsibility or liability for any damages you may experience as a result of following recipes, instructions, tips or advice in this publication.

While we hope this publication helps you find new ways to eat delicious foods, you may not always achieve the results desired due to variations in ingredients, cooking temperatures, typos, errors, omissions or individual cooking abilities.

Contents

Garlic

Garlic Mushrooms

Makes 4 servings

- **1 package (16 ounces) sliced mushrooms**
- **2 tablespoons olive oil**
- **1 teaspoon garlic powder**
- **1 teaspoon Italian seasoning**
- **½ teaspoon salt**
- **¼ teaspoon black pepper**
- **2 tablespoons chopped fresh parsley**

1. Heat large skillet over medium-high heat. Add mushrooms; cook about 10 minutes or until mushrooms are tender and have released their liquid.
2. Add oil, garlic powder, Italian seasoning, salt and pepper; cook and stir 1 minute until mushrooms are coated.
3. Transfer mushrooms to serving bowl; sprinkle with parsley.

Garlic Parmesan Spaghetti Squash

Makes 2 servings

- **3 tablespoons olive oil, divided**
- **1 medium spaghetti squash (2 to 2½ pounds)**
- **¼ teaspoon plus ⅛ teaspoon salt, divided**
- **2 cloves garlic, minced**
- **¼ teaspoon red pepper flakes**
- **⅛ teaspoon black pepper**
- **½ cup shredded Parmesan cheese**
- **⅓ cup chopped fresh parsley**

1. Preheat oven to 400°F. Brush baking sheet with 1 teaspoon oil. Cut squash in half; remove and discard seeds. Brush each cut side with 1 teaspoon oil and sprinkle each half with ⅛ teaspoon salt. Place squash cut sides down on prepared baking sheet.
2. Bake 30 to 40 minutes or until squash is fork-tender.
3. Remove squash to plate; let stand until cool enough to handle. Use fork to shred squash into long strands, reserving shells for serving, if desired.
4. Heat remaining 2 tablespoons oil in large nonstick skillet over medium-high heat. Add garlic, remaining ⅛ teaspoon salt, red pepper flakes and black pepper; cook and stir 2 to 3 minutes or until garlic begins to turn golden. Remove from heat. Add squash, cheese and parsley to skillet; stir gently just until blended. Serve immediately.

Butter Chicken

Makes 4 to 6 servings

- 2 tablespoons butter
- 1 onion, chopped
- 4 cloves garlic, minced
- 1 teaspoon minced fresh ginger
- 1 teaspoon ground turmeric
- 1 teaspoon ground coriander
- 1 teaspoon garam masala
- 1 teaspoon ground cumin
- ½ teaspoon ground red pepper
- ½ teaspoon sweet paprika
- 1 can (about 14 ounces) diced tomatoes
- ¾ teaspoon salt
- 2 pounds boneless skinless chicken breasts, cut into 2-inch pieces
- ½ cup whipping cream
- Chopped fresh cilantro
- 3 cups hot cooked basmati rice

1. Melt butter in large saucepan over medium-high heat. Add onion; cook and stir about 5 minutes or until onion begins to turn golden. Add garlic and ginger; cook and stir 1 minute. Add turmeric, coriander, garam masala, cumin, red pepper and paprika; cook and stir 30 seconds. Add tomatoes and salt; cook and stir 2 minutes. Stir in chicken; mix well.

2. Reduce heat to low; cover and simmer 20 minutes or until chicken is no longer pink in center and cooked through (165°F).

3. Stir in cream; cook 2 minutes or until heated through, stirring occasionally. Sprinkle with cilantro; serve with rice.

Garlic Knots

Makes 20 knots

- 1 package (¼ ounce) active dry yeast
- 1 teaspoon sugar
- ¾ cup warm water (105° to 115°F)
- 2¼ cups all-purpose flour
- 2 tablespoons olive oil, divided
- 1½ teaspoons salt, divided
- 4 tablespoons (½ stick) butter, divided
- 1 tablespoon minced garlic
- ¼ teaspoon garlic powder
- ½ cup grated Parmesan cheese
- 2 tablespoons chopped fresh parsley
- ½ teaspoon dried oregano

1. Dissolve yeast and sugar in warm water in large bowl of stand mixer; let stand 5 minutes or until bubbly. Add flour, 1 tablespoon oil and 1 teaspoon salt; knead with dough hook at low speed 5 minutes or until dough is smooth and elastic.
2. Shape dough into a ball. Place dough in greased bowl; turn to grease top. Cover and let rise in warm place 1 hour or until doubled in size.
3. Melt 2 tablespoons butter in small saucepan over low heat. Add remaining 1 tablespoon oil, ½ teaspoon salt, minced garlic and garlic powder; cook over very low heat 5 minutes. Pour into small bowl; set aside.
4. Preheat oven to 400°F. Line baking sheet with parchment paper.
5. Punch down dough. Turn out dough onto lightly floured surface; let rest 10 minutes. Roll out dough into 10×8-inch rectangle; cut into 20 (2-inch) squares. Roll each piece into 8-inch rope; tie in a knot. Place knots on prepared baking sheet; brush with butter mixture.
6. Bake 10 minutes or until lightly browned. Meanwhile, melt remaining 2 tablespoons butter. Combine cheese, parsley and oregano in small bowl; mix well. Brush melted butter over knots immediately after baking; sprinkle with cheese mixture. Cool slightly; serve warm.

Forty-Clove Chicken

Makes 4 to 6 servings

- 1 cut-up whole chicken (about 3 to 4 pounds)
- Salt and black pepper
- ¼ cup olive oil
- 40 cloves garlic (about 2 heads), peeled
- 4 stalks celery, thickly sliced
- ½ cup dry white wine
- ¼ cup dry vermouth
- Grated peel and juice of 1 lemon
- 2 tablespoons finely chopped fresh parsley
- 2 teaspoons dried basil
- 1 teaspoon dried oregano
- Pinch red pepper flakes

1. Preheat oven to 375°F.
2. Season chicken all over with salt and pepper. Heat oil in Dutch oven over medium-high heat. Add chicken; cook until browned on all sides.
3. Combine garlic, celery, wine, vermouth, lemon juice, parsley, basil, oregano and red pepper flakes in medium bowl; pour over chicken. Sprinkle with lemon peel.
4. Cover and bake 40 minutes. Remove cover; bake 15 minutes or until chicken is cooked through (165°F). Season to taste with salt and pepper.

Crispy Garlic-Parmesan Chicken Wings

Makes about 6 servings

- **2 pounds chicken wings (about 15 wings)**
- **2 heads garlic, separated into cloves and peeled***
- **1 cup olive oil**
- **1 teaspoon hot pepper sauce**
- **1 cup grated Parmesan cheese**
- **1 cup Italian-style dry bread crumbs**
- **1 teaspoon black pepper**
- **Ranch or blue cheese dressing (optional)**

****To easily peel whole heads of garlic, drop garlic heads into boiling water for 5 to 10 seconds. Immediately remove garlic with slotted spoon. Plunge garlic into cold water; drain. Peel away skins.***

1. Preheat oven to 375°F. Spray 13×9-inch baking pan with nonstick cooking spray. Remove and discard wing tips. Cut each wing in half at joint.
2. Place garlic, oil and hot pepper sauce in food processor; process until smooth. Pour garlic mixture into shallow bowl. Combine cheese, bread crumbs and black pepper in another shallow bowl.
3. Working with one at a time, dip wings into garlic mixture, then roll in crumb mixture, coating evenly.
4. Arrange wings in single layer in prepared pan. Drizzle remaining garlic mixture over wings; sprinkle with remaining crumb mixture.
5. Bake 45 minutes to 1 hour or until wings are cooked through, browned and crisp. Serve with ranch dressing, if desired.

Tomatoes Stuffed with Garlic Potato Salad

Makes 6 servings

- 1 pound baking potatoes, peeled and cut into ¼-inch cubes
- 3 tablespoons red or white wine vinegar, divided
- ½ cup mayonnaise
- 2 tablespoons minced fresh parsley, plus additional for garnish
- 2 cloves garlic, minced
- 1 teaspoon salt
- ⅛ teaspoon ground white pepper
- 12 large (2-inch diameter) Campari tomatoes *or* 6 plum tomatoes
- Paprika (optional)

1. For potato salad, place potatoes in medium saucepan; cover with cold water and bring to a boil over medium-high heat. Reduce heat and simmer 6 minutes or until potatoes are fork-tender. Drain and place in medium bowl. Sprinkle with 2 tablespoons vinegar; stir gently to mix. Cool slightly.
2. Gently stir in mayonnaise, 2 tablespoons parsley, remaining 1 tablespoon vinegar, garlic, salt and white pepper. Cover and refrigerate about 2 hours or until cold.
3. Cut small slice from bottom of each tomato* to allow tomatoes to stand upright. Cut top off each tomato; scoop out pulp. Discard pulp.
4. Fill each tomato with 2 to 3 tablespoons potato salad. Garnish with paprika and additional parsley. Serve immediately.

**When using plum tomatoes, cut small slice from top and bottom of tomatoes, then cut them crosswise in half. Scoop out pulp.*

Pork Meatballs in Garlicky Almond Sauce

Makes 6 servings

- ½ cup blanched whole almonds
- 1 cup chicken broth
- ⅓ cup roasted red pepper
- 4 teaspoons minced garlic, divided
- 1 teaspoon salt, divided
- ½ teaspoon saffron threads (optional)
- 1 cup fresh bread crumbs, divided
- ¼ cup dry white wine or chicken broth
- 1 pound ground pork
- ¼ cup finely chopped onion
- 1 egg
- 3 tablespoons minced fresh parsley

1. Preheat oven to 350°F. Line baking pans with foil; spray with nonstick cooking spray.
2. For sauce, place almonds in food processor; process until finely ground. Add broth, red pepper, 2 teaspoons garlic, ½ teaspoon salt and saffron, if desired; process until smooth. Stir in ¼ cup bread crumbs.
3. Place ¾ cup bread crumbs in large bowl; sprinkle with wine and stir gently. Add pork, onion, egg, parsley, remaining 2 teaspoons garlic and ½ teaspoon salt; mix well. Shape pork mixture into 24 (1-inch) balls. Arrange meatballs in baking pans, spacing about 1 inch apart. Bake about 20 minutes or until lightly browned.
4. Transfer meatballs to 2-quart baking dish. Pour sauce over meatballs. Bake 25 to 30 minutes or until sauce is bubbly.

Baked Chicken and Garlic Orzo

Makes 4 servings

- 2 tablespoons olive oil, divided
- 4 bone-in chicken breasts, skin removed
- ¼ cup dry white wine
- 10 ounces uncooked orzo
- 1 cup chopped onion
- 4 cloves garlic, minced
- 2 tablespoons chopped fresh parsley
- 1 teaspoon salt
- 1 teaspoon dried oregano
- 1 can (about 14 ounces) chicken broth
- ¼ cup water
- 1 teaspoon lemon-pepper seasoning
- Paprika
- 1 lemon, cut into 8 wedges

1. Preheat oven to 350°F. Spray 9-inch square baking dish with nonstick cooking spray.
2. Heat 1 tablespoon oil in large nonstick skillet over medium-high heat. Add chicken; cook 3 to 5 minutes or until lightly browned. Transfer to plate.
3. Add wine to skillet; cook over medium-low heat 1 minute or until slightly reduced, scraping up browned bits from bottom of skillet. Stir in orzo, onion, garlic, parsley, salt and oregano; cook and stir 1 minute. Add broth and water; mix well. Spread in prepared baking dish. Place chicken on top of orzo mixture; sprinkle with lemon-pepper and paprika.
4. Bake, uncovered, 1 hour and 10 minutes or until chicken is browned and cooked through (165°F) and orzo is tender. Drizzle remaining 1 tablespoon oil over top; serve with lemon wedges.

Lemon and Garlic Shrimp

Makes 6 to 8 servings

- ¼ cup olive oil
- 2 tablespoons butter
- 1 pound large raw shrimp, peeled and deveined (with tails on)
- 3 cloves garlic
- 2 tablespoons lemon juice
- ½ teaspoon salt
- ½ teaspoon sweet paprika
- Black pepper
- 2 tablespoons finely chopped fresh Italian parsley
- Crusty bread, sliced

1 Heat oil and butter in large skillet over medium-high heat until butter melts and mixture sizzles. Add shrimp and garlic; cook and stir 4 to 5 minutes or until shrimp are pink and opaque.

2 Add lemon juice, salt, paprika and pepper; cook and stir 1 minute. Remove from heat; discard garlic. Spoon shrimp and skillet juices into large serving bowl. Sprinkle with parsley. Serve with crusty bread for dipping.

Crispy Garlic Bites

Makes about 24 bites

- ½ (16-ounce) package frozen phyllo dough, thawed to room temperature
- ¾ cup (1½ sticks) butter, melted
- 3 large heads garlic, separated into cloves, peeled
- ½ cup finely chopped walnuts
- 1 cup Italian-style bread crumbs

1. Preheat oven to 350°F. Remove phyllo from package; unroll and place on large sheet of waxed paper. Cut phyllo crosswise into 2-inch-wide strips. Cover phyllo with large sheet of plastic wrap and clean damp kitchen towel.
2. Lay one strip of phyllo on work surface and brush with melted butter. Place 1 garlic clove at end. Sprinkle 1 teaspoon walnuts along length of strip. Roll up garlic clove and walnuts in strip, tucking in side edges as you roll. Brush with butter; roll in bread crumbs. Repeat with remaining phyllo, garlic, walnuts and butter.
3. Place on rack in shallow roasting pan. Bake 20 minutes or until coating is golden brown and garlic is tender.

Cumin

Chickpea Tikka Masala

Makes 4 servings

- 1 tablespoon olive oil
- 1 onion, chopped
- 3 cloves garlic, minced
- 1 tablespoon minced fresh ginger
- 1 tablespoon garam masala
- 1 teaspoon ground cumin
- 1 teaspoon ground coriander
- 1 teaspoon salt
- ¼ teaspoon ground red pepper
- 2 cans (about 15 ounces each) chickpeas, drained
- 1 can (28 ounces) crushed tomatoes
- 1 can (about 13 ounces) coconut milk
- 1 package (about 12 ounces) firm silken tofu, drained and cut into 1-inch cubes
- Hot cooked basmati rice
- Chopped fresh cilantro (optional)

1. Heat oil in large saucepan over medium-high heat. Add onion; cook and stir 5 minutes or until translucent. Add garlic, ginger, garam masala, cumin, coriander, salt and red pepper; cook and stir 1 minute.
2. Stir in chickpeas, tomatoes and coconut milk. Reduce heat to medium; simmer 30 minutes or until sauce is thickened and chickpeas have softened slightly.
3. Add tofu; stir gently. Cook 7 to 10 minutes or until tofu is heated through. Serve over rice; garnish with cilantro.

Fried Cauliflower with Garlic Tahini Sauce

Makes 8 servings

Sauce

- ½ cup tahini
- ¼ cup plain Greek yogurt
- 2 tablespoons lemon juice
- 2 cloves garlic, minced
- ¼ teaspoon salt
- 6 tablespoons cold water
- 1 tablespoon minced fresh parsley

Cauliflower

- 1 cup all-purpose flour
- 1½ teaspoons salt, divided
- ¼ teaspoon black pepper
- 4 eggs
- ¼ cup water
- 2 cups panko bread crumbs
- 1 teaspoon ground cumin
- 1 teaspoon garlic powder
- ¼ teaspoon ground nutmeg
- 1 large head cauliflower (2½ pounds), cut into 1-inch florets
- 1 quart vegetable oil

1. For sauce, whisk tahini, yogurt, lemon juice, garlic and ¼ teaspoon salt in medium bowl. Whisk in enough water in thin steady stream until sauce is thinned to desired consistency. Stir in parsley.
2. For cauliflower, whisk flour, ½ teaspoon salt and pepper in large bowl. Whisk eggs and ¼ cup water in medium bowl. Combine panko, remaining 1 teaspoon salt, cumin, garlic powder and nutmeg in large bowl. Toss cauliflower florets into flour mixture to coat; tap off excess. Dip in egg mixture, letting excess drain back into bowl. Place in panko mixture; toss until coated. Place breaded cauliflower on large baking sheet.
3. Line another large baking sheet with three layers of paper towels. Heat oil in large saucepan or Dutch oven over medium-high heat to 350°F; adjust heat to maintain temperature during cooking.
4. Cook cauliflower in batches 4 minutes or until golden brown and tender, stirring once or twice. Drain on prepared baking sheet. Serve warm with sauce.

Fasolada (Greek White Bean Soup)

Makes 4 to 6 servings

- 4 tablespoons olive oil, divided
- 1 large onion, diced
- 3 stalks celery, diced
- 3 carrots, diced
- 4 cloves garlic, minced
- ¼ cup tomato paste
- 1 teaspoon salt
- 1 teaspoon dried oregano
- 1 teaspoon ground cumin
- ¼ teaspoon black pepper
- 1 bay leaf
- 4 cups vegetable broth
- 3 cans (15 ounces each) cannellini beans, rinsed and drained
- 2 tablespoons lemon juice
- ¼ cup minced fresh parsley

1. Heat 2 tablespoons oil in large saucepan over medium-high heat. Add onion, celery and carrots; cook and stir 8 to 10 minutes or until vegetables are softened. Add garlic; cook and stir 30 seconds. Add tomato paste, salt, oregano, cumin, pepper and bay leaf; cook and stir 30 seconds.

2. Stir in broth; bring to a boil. Stir in beans; return to a boil. Reduce heat to medium-low; simmer 30 minutes, stirring occasionally. Stir in remaining 2 tablespoons oil and lemon juice. Remove and discard bay leaf. Sprinkle with parsley just before serving.

Vegetable Empanadas

Makes 8 servings

- 2 tablespoons olive oil
- 1 cup frozen diced hash brown potatoes
- 1 red bell pepper, chopped
- 1 green bell pepper, chopped
- 1 onion, chopped
- 1 package (8 ounces) sliced mushrooms
- 2 teaspoons minced garlic
- 1½ teaspoons ground cumin
- ½ teaspoon salt
- ½ teaspoon ground nutmeg
- ½ teaspoon black pepper
- ¼ teaspoon ground red pepper
- 1 package (17 ounces) frozen puff pastry sheets, thawed
- ½ cup (2 ounces) shredded Monterey Jack cheese
- 3 tablespoons milk
- Salsa

1. Heat oil in large nonstick skillet over medium heat. Add potatoes, bell peppers, onion, mushrooms, garlic, cumin, salt, nutmeg, black pepper and red pepper; cook and stir 5 minutes. Let cool to room temperature.
2. Preheat oven to 400°F. Unfold pastry sheets on floured surface. Roll each sheet into 12-inch square with lightly floured rolling pin; cut each sheet into four squares with sharp knife. Place about ¼ cup filling in corner of each square; sprinkle with 1 tablespoon cheese.
3. Brush small amount of milk on edges of pastry squares. Fold over opposite corners, forming triangles. Press edges with fork to seal. Cut small slit in top of each triangle with knife. At this point, empanadas may be covered and refrigerated up to 24 hours or frozen up to 1 month.
4. Place triangles on ungreased baking sheets; brush tops with remaining milk. Bake 15 to 20 minutes or until puffed and golden. Serve with salsa.

Note

Empanadas can be made and baked 2 days ahead. Reheat for 10 minutes in 400°F oven.

Honey-Citrus Chicken with Fruit Salsa

Makes 6 servings

Chicken

- ⅓ cup honey
- 3 tablespoons olive oil
- 1 teaspoon grated lemon peel
- 1 teaspoon grated lime peel
- Juice of 1 lemon
- Juice of 1 lime
- 1 teaspoon salt
- 1 teaspoon ground cumin
- ⅛ teaspoon ground red pepper or to taste
- 6 boneless skinless chicken breasts (about 6 ounces each)

Salsa

- 1 orange
- 2 cups coarsely chopped fresh pineapple
- ½ cup orange juice
- Juice of 1 lime
- 1 teaspoon grated lime peel
- 1 jalapeño pepper, seeded and minced
- Salt and black pepper
- 2 tablespoons chopped fresh cilantro

1. For marinade, combine honey, oil, lemon and lime peel, lemon and lime juices, 1 teaspoon salt, cumin and ground red pepper in large bowl; reserve 2 tablespoons marinade in small bowl. Add chicken to remaining marinade in large bowl; stir to coat. Cover and marinate at least 1 hour or up to 24 hours in refrigerator, stirring once or twice.

2. For salsa, grate 1 tablespoon orange peel; peel orange and coarsely chop. Combine grated orange peel, chopped orange, pineapple, orange juice, lime juice and peel and jalapeño in medium bowl; season to taste with salt and black pepper. Cover and refrigerate up to 24 hours.

3. Preheat broiler. Remove chicken from marinade, discarding marinade. Place chicken on broiler pan. Broil about 6 inches from heat 4 minutes per side or until chicken is cooked through (165°F) and no longer pink in center, basting with 2 tablespoons reserved marinade. Stir cilantro into salsa; serve salsa over chicken.

Mujadara

Makes 6 servings

- 1 cup dried lentils, rinsed and sorted
- ¼ cup plus 1 tablespoon olive oil, divided
- 3 sweet onions, thinly sliced
- 2½ teaspoons salt, divided
- 1½ teaspoons ground cumin
- 1 teaspoon ground allspice
- 1 cinnamon stick
- 1 bay leaf
- ⅛ to ¼ teaspoon ground red pepper
- ¾ cup uncooked long grain rice, rinsed and drained
- 3 cups vegetable broth or water
- 1 cucumber
- 1 cup plain Greek yogurt or sour cream

1. Place lentils in medium saucepan; cover with water by 1 inch. Bring to a boil over medium-high heat. Reduce heat to medium-low; simmer 10 minutes. Drain and rinse under cold water.

2. Meanwhile, heat ¼ cup oil in large saucepan or Dutch oven over medium heat. Add onions and 1 teaspoon salt; cook and stir 15 minutes or until golden brown and parts are crispy. Remove most of onions to small bowl, leaving about ½ cup in saucepan.*

3. Add remaining 1 tablespoon oil to saucepan with onions; heat over medium-high heat. Add cumin, allspice, cinnamon stick, bay leaf and red pepper; cook and stir 30 seconds. Add rice; cook and stir 2 to 3 minutes or until rice is lightly toasted. Stir in broth, lentils and 1 teaspoon salt; bring to a boil. Reduce heat to low; cover and cook about 15 minutes or until broth is absorbed and rice and lentils are tender. Remove saucepan from heat. Place clean kitchen towel over top of saucepan; replace lid and let stand 5 to 10 minutes.

4. Meanwhile, peel cucumber and trim ends. Grate cucumber on large holes of box grater; squeeze out excess liquid. Place in medium bowl; stir in yogurt and remaining ½ teaspoon salt. Serve lentils and rice with reserved onions and cucumber sauce.

**If desired, continue to cook reserved onions in medium skillet over medium heat until dark golden brown.*

Black Bean Burgers

Makes 6 burgers

- 2 cans (about 15 ounces each) black beans, rinsed and drained, divided
- ¾ cup plain dry bread crumbs
- ⅔ cup finely chopped green onions
- 2 egg whites
- ¼ cup chopped fresh basil
- 2 teaspoons onion powder
- 2 teaspoons dried oregano
- 1 teaspoon baking powder
- 1 teaspoon ground cumin
- 1 teaspoon black pepper
- ½ teaspoon salt
- ¾ cup fresh or thawed frozen corn
- ¾ cup chopped roasted red pepper
- 2 tablespoons vegetable oil
- 6 whole wheat hamburger buns
- Avocado slices and salsa (optional)

1. Combine half of beans, bread crumbs, green onions, egg whites, basil, onion powder, oregano, baking powder, cumin, black pepper and salt in food processor; pulse 30 to 40 seconds or until mixture begins to hold together. Transfer to large bowl; stir in remaining beans, corn and roasted red pepper. Let stand 20 minutes to allow flavors to develop.
2. Preheat oven to 350°F. Line baking sheet with parchment paper.
3. Shape mixture into six patties. Place on prepared baking sheet; brush both sides with oil or spray with nonstick cooking spray.
4. Bake 18 to 20 minutes or until patties are firm. Serve on buns topped with avocado and salsa, if desired.

Tip

Cooked burgers can be wrapped up and frozen to save for grilling season. Grill burgers over medium-high heat until heated through.

Onion Marmalade

Makes 5 cups

- 1 bottle (12 ounces) balsamic vinegar
- 1 bottle (12 ounces) white wine vinegar
- 3 tablespoons arrowroot or cornstarch
- 2 tablespoons water
- 1½ cups packed dark brown sugar
- 2 teaspoons cumin seeds
- 2 teaspoons coriander seeds
- 4 large yellow onions, halved and thinly sliced
- 1 teaspoon salt

Slow Cooker Directions

1. With exhaust fan running, cook vinegars in large saucepan over high heat until reduced to ¼ cup. Sauce will be thick and syrupy. Remove from heat.
2. Stir arrowroot and water in small bowl until smooth. Add brown sugar, cumin, coriander and arrowroot mixture to vinegar; mix well.
3. Place onions in slow cooker. Stir in vinegar mixture and salt; mix well. Cover; cook on LOW 8 to 10 hours or HIGH 4 to 6 hours until onions are soft, stirring occasionally to prevent sticking. Store in airtight container in refrigerator for up to two weeks.

Tip

Serve as side dish or condiment with eggs, roasted vegetables and meats, and as a topping for sandwiches.

Indian-Style Chicken

Makes 4 servings

- 2 tablespoons vegetable oil, divided
- 1 pound boneless skinless chicken thighs
- 1½ cups chopped onion
- 2 teaspoons grated fresh ginger
- 1½ teaspoons ground cumin
- 3 cloves garlic, minced
- 1 can (about 14 ounces) diced tomatoes
- 2 teaspoons ground coriander
- 1 teaspoon salt
- ½ teaspoon black pepper
- ½ teaspoon ground turmeric
- ½ cup plain yogurt
- 3 cups cooked brown rice

1. Heat 1 tablespoon oil in large nonstick skillet over medium-high heat. Add chicken; cook 4 to 5 minutes or until lightly browned on both sides, turning once. Transfer chicken to plate.
2. Heat remaining 1 tablespoon oil in same skillet over medium-low heat. Add onion, ginger, cumin and garlic; cook 5 minutes, stirring occasionally. Stir in tomatoes, coriander, salt, pepper and turmeric. Bring to a boil. Reduce heat to medium; simmer, uncovered, 3 minutes, stirring occasionally.
3. Gradually stir yogurt into skillet. Return chicken to skillet. Bring to a boil. Reduce heat to medium-low; cover and simmer 12 minutes or until chicken is tender and no longer pink in center. Remove cover; simmer over medium heat 5 minutes.
4. Spoon rice into serving bowls. Top with chicken and sauce.

Middle Eastern Lentil Soup

Makes 4 servings

- 2 tablespoons olive oil
- 1 small onion, chopped
- 1 red bell pepper, chopped
- 1 teaspoon whole fennel seeds
- 1 teaspoon ground cumin
- ¼ teaspoon ground red pepper
- 4 cups water
- 1 cup dried lentils, sorted,* rinsed and drained
- 1 teaspoon salt
- 1 tablespoon lemon juice
- ½ cup plain yogurt
- 2 tablespoons chopped fresh parsley

**Packages of dried lentils may contain dirt and tiny stones. Thoroughly rinse lentils in fine-mesh strainer; sort through them and discard any unusual-looking pieces.*

1. Heat oil in large saucepan over medium-high heat. Add onion and bell pepper; cook and stir 5 minutes or until tender. Add fennel seeds, cumin and red pepper; cook and stir 1 minute.
2. Add water, lentils and salt; bring to a boil. Reduce heat to low; cover and simmer 25 to 30 minutes or until lentils are tender. Stir in lemon juice. Top each serving with yogurt; sprinkle with parsley.

Chile-Corn Quiche

Makes 6 servings

- 1 unbaked 9-inch pie crust
- 1 cup fresh or thawed frozen corn
- 1 can (4 ounces) diced mild green chiles, drained
- ¼ cup thinly sliced green onions
- 1 cup (4 ounces) shredded Monterey Jack cheese
- 1½ cups half-and-half
- 3 eggs
- 1 teaspoon ground cumin
- ½ teaspoon salt

1 Preheat oven to 450°F. Line crust with foil; fill with dried beans or rice.* Bake 10 minutes. Remove foil and beans. Bake 5 minutes or until lightly browned. Cool slightly. *Reduce oven temperature to 375°F.*

2 Combine corn, chiles and green onions in small bowl. Spoon into crust; top with cheese. Whisk half-and-half, eggs, cumin and salt in medium bowl; pour over cheese.

3 Bake 35 to 45 minutes or until filling is puffed and knife inserted into center comes out clean. Let stand 10 minutes before serving.

**Baking a crust with dried beans or rice helps hold its shape before adding in the filling. Discard beans or rice afterwards.*

Zesty Queso Dip

Makes 3 cups

- 1 package (16 ounces) pasteurized process cheese product, cubed
- 1 can (10 ounces) diced tomatoes with green chiles
- 1 cup sliced green onions
- 2 teaspoons ground coriander
- 2 teaspoons ground cumin
- ¾ teaspoon hot pepper sauce
- Jalapeño pepper slices (optional)
- Tortilla chips

1. Combine cheese, tomatoes, green onions, coriander, cumin and hot pepper sauce in medium saucepan. Cook over low heat 10 to 15 minutes or until mixture is hot and smooth, stirring frequently.
2. Pour into serving bowl; garnish with jalapeño pepper slices. Serve with tortilla chips.

Spanish Ham and Cheese Toasts

Makes 24 appetizers

- 1 package (about 5 ounces) goat cheese, at room temperature
- 1 teaspoon ground cumin
- ½ teaspoon smoked or sweet paprika
- 24 (½-inch) toasted French bread slices
- ½ cup chopped fresh parsley
- 8 slices Serrano ham or proscuitto, cut crosswise into thirds

1. Place goat cheese in small bowl. Add cumin and paprika; stir until well blended and uniform in color. Cover and let stand 30 minutes.
2. Spread goat cheese mixture on toasts; sprinkle with parsley. Top each toast with one piece of ham. Serve at room temperature.

Tip

The goat cheese mixture can be prepared up to 2 days in advance. Remove from the refrigerator 30 minutes before assembling the toasts.

Chili Powder

Turkey Sloppy Joes

Makes 8 servings

- 1 cup ketchup
- 2 tablespoons packed brown sugar
- 2 tablespoons Worcestershire sauce
- 2 tablespoons yellow mustard
- 2 tablespoons cider vinegar
- 1 tablespoon vegetable oil
- 2 pounds ground turkey
- 1 medium onion, chopped
- 1 red bell pepper, chopped
- 1 clove garlic, minced
- 2 teaspoons chili powder
- ½ teaspoon salt
- ½ teaspoon ground cumin
- ¼ teaspoon black pepper
- 8 hamburger buns

1. Combine ketchup, brown sugar, Worcestershire sauce, mustard and vinegar in medium bowl.
2. Heat oil in large skillet over medium-high heat. Add turkey, onion, bell pepper and garlic; cook and stir 10 minutes or until turkey is no longer pink, stirring to break up meat. Add chili powder, salt, cumin and black pepper; cook and stir 1 minute.
3. Add ketchup mixture; mix well. Cook 10 minutes, stirring occasionally. Serve on buns.

Southwestern Chicken Chili

Makes 6 servings

1 tablespoon vegetable oil
1 small onion, chopped
1 small red bell pepper, diced (¼-inch pieces)
1 jalapeño pepper, finely chopped
6 cloves garlic, minced
3 tablespoons all-purpose flour
2 tablespoons chili powder
1 tablespoon ground cumin
2 teaspoons salt
1 can (about 15 ounces) kidney beans, rinsed and drained
1 can (about 14 ounces) chicken broth
1 can (8 ounces) tomato sauce
1 can (4 ounces) diced green chiles
2 tablespoons chopped fresh cilantro
3 cups shredded cooked chicken
Optional toppings: shredded Cheddar cheese, chopped red onion and/or tortilla chips

1 Heat oil in large saucepan over medium heat. Add onion; cook and stir about 5 minutes or until translucent. Add bell pepper, jalapeño and garlic; cook and stir 3 minutes. Add flour, chili powder, cumin and salt; cook and stir 1 minute or until spices are fragrant.

2 Stir in beans, broth, tomato sauce, chiles and cilantro; bring to a boil. Reduce heat to low; cover and simmer 20 minutes, stirring occasionally.

3 Stir in chicken; cover and simmer 20 minutes. If chili is too thin, cook, uncovered, until slightly thickened. Serve with desired toppings.

Spanish Tapas Potatoes (Patatas Bravas)

Makes 10 to 12 servings

- 2½ pounds small red potatoes, quartered
- ⅓ cup plus 2 tablespoons olive oil, divided
- 1 teaspoon coarse salt
- ½ teaspoon dried rosemary
- 1 can (about 14 ounces) diced tomatoes
- 2 tablespoons red wine vinegar
- 1 tablespoon minced garlic
- 1 tablespoon chili powder
- 1 tablespoon sweet paprika
- ¼ teaspoon salt
- ¼ teaspoon chipotle chili powder
- ⅛ to ¼ teaspoon ground red pepper

1. Preheat oven to 425°F. Combine potatoes, 2 tablespoons oil, 1 teaspoon coarse salt and rosemary in large bowl; toss to coat. Spread in single layer on large baking sheet.
2. Roast 35 to 40 minutes or until potatoes are crisp and brown, turning every 10 minutes.
3. Meanwhile, combine tomatoes, remaining ⅓ cup oil, vinegar, garlic, chili powder, paprika, ¼ teaspoon salt, chipotle chili powder and red pepper in food processor or blender; process just until blended. Transfer to large saucepan; cover and cook over medium-high heat 5 minutes or until slightly thickened. Cool slightly.
4. Drizzle sauce over potatoes or serve sauce in separate bowl for dipping.

Texas-Style Barbecued Brisket

Makes 10 to 12 servings

- 3 tablespoons Worcestershire sauce
- 2 cloves garlic, minced
- 1 tablespoon chili powder
- 1 teaspoon celery salt
- 1 teaspoon black pepper
- 1 teaspoon liquid smoke
- 1 beef brisket (3 to 4 pounds), trimmed
- 2 bay leaves
- Barbecue Sauce (recipe follows)

Slow Cooker Directions

1 Combine Worcestershire sauce, garlic, chili powder, celery salt, pepper and liquid smoke in small bowl. Spread mixture on all sides of beef. Place beef in large resealable food storage bag; seal bag. Refrigerate 24 hours.

2 Place beef, marinade and bay leaves in slow cooker, cutting meat in half to fit, if necessary. Cover; cook on LOW 7 hours. Meanwhile, prepare Barbecue Sauce.

3 Remove beef from slow cooker and pour juices into 2-cup measure; let stand 5 minutes. Skim fat from juices. Remove and discard bay leaves. Stir 1 cup juices into Barbecue Sauce. Discard remaining juices.

4 Return beef and sauce mixture to slow cooker. Cover; cook on LOW 1 hour or until beef is fork-tender. Remove beef to cutting board. Cut across grain into ¼-inch-thick slices. Serve with Barbecue Sauce.

Barbecue Sauce

Makes about 1¾ cups

- 2 tablespoons vegetable oil
- 1 onion, chopped
- 2 cloves garlic, minced
- 1 cup ketchup
- ½ cup molasses
- ¼ cup cider vinegar
- 2 teaspoons chili powder
- ½ teaspoon dry mustard

1 Heat oil in medium saucepan over medium heat. Add onion and garlic; cook and stir 5 minutes or until onion is tender.

2 Stir in ketchup, molasses, vinegar, chili powder and mustard; simmer over medium heat 5 minutes.

Four Bean Chili

Makes 8 to 10 servings

- 2 tablespoons olive oil
- 1 onion, finely chopped
- 2 medium carrots, chopped
- 1 red bell pepper, chopped
- 3 tablespoons chili powder
- 2 tablespoons ground cumin
- 2 tablespoons tomato paste
- 2 tablespoons packed dark brown sugar
- 3 cloves garlic, minced
- 1 tablespoon dried oregano
- 1 teaspoon salt
- 1 can (28 ounces) diced tomatoes
- 1 can (15 ounces) tomato sauce
- 1 can (about 15 ounces) small white beans, rinsed and drained
- 1 can (about 15 ounces) light kidney beans, rinsed and drained
- 1 can (about 15 ounces) dark kidney beans, rinsed and drained
- 1 can (about 15 ounces) pinto beans, rinsed and drained
- 1 cup vegetable broth or water
- 1 can (4 ounces) diced mild green chiles
- 1 ounce unsweetened chocolate, chopped
- 1 tablespoon cider vinegar

1. Heat oil in large saucepan or Dutch oven over medium-high heat. Add onion, carrots and bell pepper; cook 10 minutes or until vegetables are tender, stirring frequently. Add chili powder, cumin, tomato paste, brown sugar, garlic, oregano and salt; cook and stir 1 minute.

2. Stir in tomatoes, tomato sauce, beans, broth, chiles and chocolate; bring to a boil. Reduce heat to medium; simmer 20 minutes, stirring occasionally. Stir in vinegar just before serving.

Mexican Shrimp with Hot Chili Pepper Butter

Makes 4 servings

- 2 tablespoons olive oil
- 2 cloves garlic, minced
- 1 cup chopped onions
- 2 pounds large shrimp, peeled and deveined
- ¼ cup chili powder
- ¼ teaspoon ground red pepper
- ½ cup (1 stick) butter, cut into pieces
- ¼ cup lime juice (about 2 limes)
- ¾ teaspoon salt
- 3 cups hot cooked white rice or yellow Spanish rice
- Lime wedges

1. Heat 1 tablespoon oil in large nonstick skillet or wok over medium-high heat. Add 1 clove garlic; cook 15 seconds. Add ½ cup onion and 1 pound shrimp. Sprinkle with half of chili powder and red pepper; cook 5 minutes or until shrimp are opaque. Transfer to large bowl; repeat with remaining oil, garlic, shrimp, chili powder and red pepper.
2. Return reserved shrimp mixture to skillet. Add butter, lime juice and salt; cook and stir until butter is melted.
3. Place rice on serving platter. Spoon shrimp mixture over rice. Garnish with lime wedges.

Grilled Pork Chops with Lager Barbecue Sauce

Makes 4 servings

- 1 cup lager
- ⅓ cup maple syrup
- 3 tablespoons molasses
- 1 tablespoon Mexican-style hot chili powder
- 4 bone-in center-cut pork chops, 1 inch thick (2 to 2¼ pounds)
- Lager Barbecue Sauce (recipe follows)
- ¾ teaspoon salt
- ¼ teaspoon black pepper

1. Combine lager, maple syrup, molasses, chili powder and pork chops in medium bowl. Place pork chops in baking dish or large food storage container. Pour sauce over pork; turn to coat. Cover and marinate in refrigerator 2 hours, turning occasionally.
2. Meanwhile, prepare Lager Barbecue Sauce.
3. Oil grill grate. Prepare grill for direct cooking over medium-high heat.
4. Remove pork chops from marinade; discard marinade. Sprinkle with salt and pepper. Grill 6 to 7 minutes per side or until 160°F. Serve with Lager Barbecue Sauce.

Lager Barbecue Sauce

Makes about ½ cup

- ½ cup lager
- ⅓ cup ketchup
- 3 tablespoons maple syrup
- 2 tablespoons finely chopped onion
- 1 tablespoon molasses
- 1 tablespoon cider vinegar
- ½ teaspoon Mexican-style hot chili powder

1. Combine lager, ketchup, maple syrup, onion, molasses, vinegar and chili powder in small saucepan. Bring to a simmer over medium heat.
2. Cook 10 to 12 minutes or until slightly thickened, stirring occasionally.

Mexican-Style Corn on the Cob

Makes 4 servings

- ¼ cup mayonnaise
- 2 teaspoons chili powder
- 1 teaspoon grated lime peel
- 4 ears corn, shucked
- ¼ cup grated Parmesan or cotija cheese

1. Prepare grill for direct cooking over medium-high heat. Combine mayonnaise, chili powder and lime peel in small bowl; set aside.

2. Grill corn, uncovered, 4 to 6 minutes or until lightly charred, turning three times. Spread mayonnaise mixture over corn; sprinkle with cheese.

Chili Cashews

Makes 2 cups

- 1 tablespoon vegetable oil
- 2 teaspoons chili powder
- 1 teaspoon ground cumin
- ½ teaspoon sugar
- ½ teaspoon red pepper flakes
- 2 cups roasted salted whole cashews (about 9 ounces)

1. Preheat oven to 350°F. Line baking sheet with foil; spray foil with nonstick cooking spray.
2. Combine oil, chili powder, cumin, sugar and red pepper flakes in medium bowl; stir until well blended. Add cashews, stirring to coat evenly. Spread mixture in single layer on prepared baking sheet.
3. Bake 8 to 10 minutes or until golden, stirring once. Cool completely on baking sheet.

Spicy Chocolate-Frosted Cinnamon Cupcakes

Makes 24 cupcakes

- 2½ cups all-purpose flour
- 1 teaspoon baking soda
- 1 teaspoon baking powder
- 1 teaspoon ground cinnamon
- ½ teaspoon salt
- ⅛ teaspoon ground nutmeg
- 1½ cups granulated sugar
- ¾ cup (1½ sticks) butter, softened
- 3 eggs
- 2 tablespoons vegetable oil
- 1½ teaspoons vanilla
- 1 container (7 ounces) plain Greek yogurt
- Spicy Chocolate Frosting (recipe follows)
- Chocolate curls (optional)

1. Preheat oven to 350°F. Line 24 standard (2½-inch) muffin cups with paper baking cups. Whisk flour, baking soda, baking powder, cinnamon, salt and nutmeg in medium bowl.
2. Beat granulated sugar and butter in large bowl with electric mixer at medium speed until creamy. Add eggs, oil and vanilla, beating until well blended. Alternately add flour mixture and yogurt, beating at low speed after each addition. Spoon batter evenly into prepared muffin cups.
3. Bake 18 minutes or until toothpick inserted into centers comes out clean. Cool in pans 5 minutes. Remove to wire racks; cool completely.
4. Meanwhile, prepare Spicy Chocolate Frosting. Pipe or spread onto cupcakes. Garnish with chocolate curls.

Spicy Chocolate Frosting

Beat 2 cups (4 sticks) softened butter in large bowl with electric mixer at medium speed until creamy. Add 4 cups powdered sugar, ¼ cup milk, 1 teaspoon ground cinnamon, 1 teaspoon ancho chile powder, 1 teaspoon vanilla and ½ teaspoon ground red pepper; beat at medium-high speed 5 minutes or until light and fluffy. Beat in 10 ounces cooled melted bittersweet (70%) chocolate until blended. Makes about 4 cups.

Mixed Berry Cobbler with Chili Cornbread Topping

Makes 6 to 8 servings

Filling

- 2 cups thawed frozen cranberries
- 2 cups fresh blueberries
- 2 cups fresh raspberries
- 1 cup sugar
- 3 tablespoons cornstarch
- 1 tablespoon grated orange peel

Cornbread Topping

- ¾ cup cornmeal
- ½ cup all-purpose flour
- 2 tablespoons sugar
- 2 teaspoons ground ancho chili powder*
- ¾ teaspoon baking powder
- ¼ teaspoon baking soda
- ¼ teaspoon salt
- ¾ cup buttermilk
- 1 egg
- 2 tablespoons butter, melted

1 Preheat oven to 400°F. Spray 8-inch square baking dish with nonstick cooking spray.

2 For filling, combine cranberries, blueberries, raspberries, 1 cup sugar, cornstarch and orange peel in medium bowl; toss to coat. Spoon into prepared baking dish.

3 For topping, combine cornmeal, flour, 2 tablespoons sugar, chili powder, baking powder, baking soda and salt in medium bowl; mix well. Add buttermilk, egg and melted butter; stir just until moistened. Pour batter over fruit mixture, spreading evenly and leaving small border (about ½ inch) around edges of baking dish.

4 Bake about 35 minutes or until filling is thick and bubbly and cornbread topping is golden brown. Let stand 30 minutes before serving.

**If ancho chili powder is unavailable, substitute regular chili powder.*

Paprika

Roasted Red Potatoes

Makes 4 servings

- 2 pounds unpeeled small red potatoes, cut into halves (or quarters if larger than 1 inch)
- 2 tablespoons olive oil
- 1 teaspoon salt
- ¾ teaspoon smoked paprika
- ¼ teaspoon black pepper

1. Preheat oven to 425°F. Spray baking sheet with nonstick cooking spray.
2. Combine potatoes, oil, salt, paprika and pepper in medium bowl; toss to coat. Spread potatoes cut sides down in single layer on prepared baking sheet.
3. Roast 25 minutes or until bottoms are browned. Turn and roast 10 minutes or until potatoes are tender.

Crispy Breaded Mushroom "Wings"

Makes 4 servings

- ¼ cup panko bread crumbs
- 2 teaspoons garlic powder
- 1½ teaspoons poultry seasoning
- 1½ teaspoons celery seed
- 1½ teaspoons sweet or smoked paprika
- 1 teaspoon onion powder
- ½ teaspoon dried thyme
- ½ teaspoon sage
- ½ teaspoon chili powder
- ½ cup all-purpose flour
- 1 cup buttermilk
- 2 cups oyster mushrooms
- Blue cheese or ranch dressing

1. Preheat oven to 425°F. Line baking sheet with parchment paper.
2. Combine panko, garlic powder, poultry seasoning, celery seed, paprika, onion powder, thyme, sage and chili powder in medium bowl. Place flour in large bowl; slowly whisk in buttermilk until well blended and smooth.
3. Use fork to dip mushrooms into buttermilk mixture; roll in panko mixture to coat. Place on prepared baking sheet.
4. Bake 15 minutes; turn and bake 5 to 10 minutes or until mushrooms are browned and crispy. Serve with dressing for dipping.

Harissa Honey Chicken and Rice Bowls

Makes 4 servings

- 4 tablespoons olive oil, divided
- 3 tablespoons harissa
- 2 tablespoons honey, divided
- 2 tablespoons lemon juice
- 3 cloves garlic, minced
- 1½ teaspoons smoked paprika
- 1 teaspoon salt
- 1 teaspoon ground coriander
- ½ teaspoon ground cumin
- 1½ pounds boneless skinless chicken thighs (4 to 6)
- 3 cups hot cooked basmati rice
- 1 cup halved grape tomatoes
- 1 cucumber, finely diced
- 1 cup shredded red cabbage
- 1 cup crumbled feta cheese
- ¼ cup chopped green onions

1. Combine 2 tablespoons oil, harissa, 1 tablespoon honey, lemon juice, garlic, paprika, salt, coriander and cumin in small bowl; mix well.
2. Place chicken in large resealable food storage bag. Pour harissa mixture over chicken; seal bag and massage marinade into chicken. Marinate in refrigerator at least 1 hour or up to 8 hours.
3. Remove chicken from refrigerator 30 minutes before cooking. Heat remaining 2 tablespoons oil in large skillet over medium-high heat. Add chicken in single layer; cook about 8 minutes or until browned. Turn and cook 8 minutes or until cooked through (165°F). Brush chicken with remaining 1 tablespoon honey, turning to coat both sides. Transfer chicken to cutting board; let stand 5 minutes.
4. Chop or slice chicken. Divide rice among four serving bowls; top with chicken, tomatoes, cucumber, cabbage, cheese and green onions.

Cheddar Onion Bites

Makes 3 dozen bites

- 2 cups all-purpose flour
- 1 tablespoon sugar
- 1 teaspoon smoked paprika
- ½ teaspoon salt
- ¼ teaspoon ground cumin
- 1 cup (2 sticks) butter, softened
- 1 egg
- 1¼ cups (5 ounces) shredded sharp Cheddar cheese
- 1 cup canned French fried onions, coarsely chopped
- ¾ cup roasted salted sunflower seeds
- ½ cup bacon bits or chopped crisp-cooked bacon

1. Preheat oven to 350°F. Line baking sheets with parchment paper.
2. Combine flour, sugar, paprika, salt and cumin in large bowl. Add butter; beat with electric mixer at low speed until crumbly. Add egg; beat until well blended. Stir in cheese, onions, sunflower seeds and bacon bits.
3. Shape dough by heaping tablespoonfuls into balls; place 1 inch apart on prepared baking sheets. Flatten slightly.
4. Bake 15 to 20 minutes or until edges and bottoms are light golden brown. Cool on baking sheets 5 minutes. Remove to wire rack; serve warm or cool completely. Store leftovers in airtight container.

Peri-Peri Chicken

Makes 4 servings

- 1 small red onion, coarsely chopped
- 1 roasted red pepper (about 3 ounces)
- ¼ cup olive oil
- ¼ cup lemon juice
- 2 tablespoons white vinegar
- 4 cloves garlic
- 1 tablespoon smoked paprika
- 1½ teaspoons salt
- 1½ teaspoons red pepper flakes
- 1 teaspoon dried oregano
- ½ teaspoon black pepper
- 1 cut-up whole chicken (3 to 4 pounds)

1. Combine onion, roasted pepper, oil, lemon juice, vinegar, garlic, paprika, salt, red pepper flakes, oregano and black pepper in blender or food processor; blend until smooth. Pour half of marinade into small bowl; cover and refrigerate until ready to use.

2. Use sharp knife to make several slashes in each piece of chicken (about ¼ inch deep). Place chicken in large resealable food storage bag. Pour remaining marinade over chicken; seal bag and turn to coat, massaging marinade into chicken. Marinate in refrigerator at least 4 hours or overnight, turning occasionally.

3. Remove chicken from refrigerator about 30 minutes before cooking. Preheat oven to 400°F.* Line baking sheet with foil. Drain chicken, discarding marinade. Arrange chicken on baking sheet.

4. Bake about 45 minutes or until chicken is cooked through (165°F), brushing with some of reserved marinade every 15 minutes.

**For a smokier flavor, grill chicken over medium heat 30 to 40 minutes or until cooked through (165°F).*

Pumpkin Polenta

Makes 4 servings

- **1 tablespoon olive oil**
- **1 tablespoon butter, plus additional for serving**
- **1 medium onion, chopped**
- **¾ teaspoon smoked paprika**
- **½ teaspoon salt**
- **¼ teaspoon ground mace or nutmeg**
- **⅛ teaspoon ground red pepper**
- **1 can (15 ounces) pumpkin purée**
- **2 cups vegetable broth or water**
- **1 cup milk**
- **1 cup instant polenta**
- **½ cup (2 ounces) shredded fontina cheese, plus additional for serving**

1. Heat oil and 1 tablespoon butter in medium saucepan over medium heat. Add onion; cook and stir 5 minutes or until softened. Add paprika, salt, mace and red pepper; cook 30 seconds, stirring constantly. Add pumpkin; cook 2 minutes, stirring frequently.
2. Whisk in broth and milk; bring to a boil over high heat. Stir in polenta in thin steady stream. Reduce heat to medium-high; cook 5 minutes or until very thick, stirring constantly.
3. Remove from heat; stir in ½ cup cheese until melted. Top each serving with additional butter and cheese, if desired.

Pasta Paprikash

Makes 4 to 6 servings

- 8 ounces uncooked long pasta (linguine, fettuccine or spaghetti)
- 2 medium red bell peppers
- 2 tablespoons olive oil
- 1 medium onion, thinly sliced
- 1 clove garlic, minced
- 2 tablespoons all-purpose flour
- 4 teaspoons sweet Hungarian paprika
- ½ teaspoon salt
- ¼ teaspoon black pepper
- 1 cup water or vegetable broth
- 1 can (8 ounces) tomato sauce
- ¼ cup sour cream
- Chopped fresh parsley

1. Cook pasta in large saucepan of salted boiling water according to package directions for al dente. Drain and return to saucepan; keep warm.
2. Meanwhile, cut red peppers lengthwise into thin strips; cut strips crosswise into halves.
3. Heat oil in large skillet over medium heat. Add bell peppers, onion and garlic; cook and stir 8 to 10 minutes or until peppers are very soft. Sprinkle flour, paprika, salt and black pepper over vegetables; cook and stir 2 minutes. Gradually stir in water until smooth; stir in tomato sauce. Reduce heat to low; simmer about 5 minutes or until sauce thickens.
4. Remove skillet from heat. Place sour cream in small bowl; stir in several spoonfuls hot mixture. Stir sour cream mixture into sauce in skillet. Pour sauce over pasta; stir until well blended. Sprinkle with parsley.

Grilled Tilapia with Zesty Mustard Sauce

Makes 4 servings

- 2 tablespoons butter, softened
- 1 teaspoon Dijon mustard
- ½ teaspoon grated lemon peel
- ½ teaspoon Worcestershire sauce
- ¾ teaspoon salt, divided
- ¼ teaspoon black pepper
- 4 mild thin fish fillets, such as tilapia (about 4 ounces each)
- 1½ teaspoons sweet or smoked paprika
- ½ medium lemon, quartered

1 Prepare grill for direct cooking over high heat.

2 Stir butter, mustard, lemon peel, Worcestershire sauce, ¼ teaspoon salt and pepper in small bowl until well blended.

3 Sprinkle both sides of fish with paprika and remaining ½ teaspoon salt. Lightly spray grill basket with nonstick cooking spray. Place fish in basket. Grill, covered, 3 minutes. Turn and grill, covered, 2 to 3 minutes, or until fish flakes easily when tested with fork. Transfer to serving plates.

4 Squeeze one lemon wedge over each fillet. Spread butter mixture evenly over fish.

Paprika Pork with Spinach

Makes 4 servings

1 pound boneless pork loin or leg, trimmed, cut into 1-inch cubes
3 tablespoons all-purpose flour
1 teaspoon salt
3 tablespoons vegetable oil
1 cup frozen pearl onions, thawed
1 tablespoon sweet paprika
1 can (about 14 ounces) vegetable or chicken broth
2 packages (3 ounces each) ramen noodles*
1 package (10 ounces) frozen chopped spinach, thawed and squeezed dry
½ cup sour cream
Shredded carrots (optional)

**Use any flavor; discard seasoning packets.*

1 Place pork, flour and salt in large bowl; toss until pork is well coated.

2 Heat large skillet or wok over high heat about 1 minute. Drizzle oil into skillet; heat 30 seconds. Add pork; cook and stir about 5 minutes or until well browned on all sides. Transfer pork to large bowl.

3 Add onions and paprika to skillet; cook and stir 1 minute. Stir in broth, noodles and pork; cover and bring to a boil. Reduce heat to low; cook about 8 minutes or until noodles and pork are tender, stirring occasionally.

4 Stir spinach into skillet; cover and cook until heated through, adding additional water if needed. Stir in sour cream until well blended. Garnish with shredded carrot.

Pork Chops Paprikash

Makes 4 servings

- 2 teaspoons butter
- 1 medium onion, very thinly sliced into rings
- 1¼ teaspoons sweet paprika, divided
- 1 teaspoon garlic salt
- ½ teaspoon black pepper
- 4 (5- to 6-ounce) bone-in center-cut pork chops (about ½ inch thick)
- ⅓ cup well-drained sauerkraut
- ⅓ cup sour cream

1. Preheat broiler.
2. Melt butter in large skillet over medium-high heat. Add onion; cook about 10 minutes or until golden brown and tender, stirring occasionally.
3. Meanwhile, sprinkle 1 teaspoon paprika, garlic salt and pepper over both sides of pork chops. Place chops on rack of broiler pan.
4. Broil 4 to 5 inches from heat source 5 minutes. Turn; broil 4 to 5 minutes or until chops are barely pink in center (145°F).
5. Combine onion, sauerkraut, sour cream and remaining ¼ teaspoon paprika in small bowl; mix well. Serve with pork.

Little Ribs in Paprika Sauce

Makes 6 to 8 servings

- 1 rack pork baby back ribs (about 1½ pounds), cut into individual pieces
- 1 can (about 14 ounces) chicken broth
- 1 cup dry white wine or beer
- 1 tablespoon olive oil
- 2 teaspoons dried oregano
- 2 teaspoons smoked or sweet paprika
- 4 cloves garlic, minced
- ½ teaspoon salt
- ¼ teaspoon black pepper

1. Place ribs, broth, wine, oil, oregano, paprika, garlic, salt and pepper in large saucepan. Bring to a boil over medium-high heat. Reduce heat to low; cover and simmer 1 hour or until meat is tender and begins to separate from bones.

2. Remove ribs to serving plate; keep warm. Skim and discard fat from cooking liquid. Bring to a boil over medium heat. Reduce heat to low; simmer until sauce is reduced by half. Spoon sauce over ribs.

Curry Powder

Ginger Curry Pumpkin Soup

Makes 8 servings

- 1 tablespoon vegetable oil
- 1 large sweet onion, coarsely chopped
- 1 large Golden Delicious apple, peeled and coarsely chopped
- 3 (¼-inch) slices peeled fresh ginger
- 1½ teaspoons curry powder
- 2½ to 3 cups vegetable broth, divided
- 2 cans (15 ounces each) pumpkin purée
- 1 cup half-and-half
- 1 teaspoon salt
- Black pepper
- Roasted salted pumpkin seeds (optional)

1. Heat oil in large saucepan over medium heat. Add onion, apple, ginger and curry powder; cook 10 minutes, stirring occasionally. Add ½ cup broth; cover and simmer 10 minutes or until apple is tender.
2. Blend mixture with immersion blender until smooth. (Or blend in blender or food processor and return to saucepan.)
3. Add pumpkin, 2 cups broth, half-and-half, salt and pepper to saucepan; cook until heated through, stirring occasionally. If soup is too thick, add additional broth, a few tablespoons at a time, until soup reaches desired consistency. Garnish with pumpkin seeds.

Sweet Curried Chicken and Quinoa Salad

Makes 2 servings

- ⅓ cup uncooked quinoa
- 1 cup water
- ¾ teaspoon salt, divided
- 2 tablespoons sliced almonds
- 1 tablespoon olive oil
- 1 boneless skinless chicken breast (about 6 ounces), cut into ½-inch cubes
- 2 tablespoons mayonnaise
- 2 tablespoons sour cream
- 2 teaspoons sugar
- 1 teaspoon curry powder
- ¼ teaspoon ground cumin
- ½ cup very thinly sliced celery
- ¼ cup finely chopped red onion
- 3 tablespoons golden raisins or regular raisins

1. Place quinoa in fine-mesh strainer; rinse well under cold water. Bring 1 cup water to a boil in small saucepan over high heat. Stir in quinoa and ½ teaspoon salt; reduce heat to medium-low. Cover and simmer 15 to 18 minutes or until liquid is absorbed and quinoa is tender. Let cool.
2. Heat large nonstick skillet over medium-high heat. Add almonds; cook and stir 3 to 4 minutes or until lightly browned. Set aside on plate. Heat oil in same skillet over medium-high heat. Add chicken; cook and stir 3 to 5 minutes or until cooked through (165°F) and no longer pink in center. Let cool.
3. Combine mayonnaise, sour cream, sugar, curry powder, cumin and remaining ¼ teaspoon salt in medium bowl; stir until well blended. Stir in celery, onion and raisins.
4. Add chicken, almonds and quinoa; stir gently until blended. Let stand 10 minutes to blend flavors.

Beans and Greens with Curry

Makes 6 servings

- 1 cup dried adzuki beans* or light red kidney beans
- 2½ teaspoons salt, divided
- 4 cups plus 2 tablespoons cold water, plus additional for soaking
- 1 tablespoon olive oil
- ½ cup diced white onion
- 2 cloves garlic, minced
- 2 teaspoons sweet or spicy curry powder
- 2 pounds Swiss chard or kale, stemmed and torn
- ¼ teaspoon black pepper

**Adzuki beans are small reddish beans with a sweet flavor and high protein content. They are used in Japanese cooking and can be found at natural food markets.*

1. Place beans and 2 teaspoons salt in medium bowl. Add enough water to cover by 2 inches. Soak overnight. Drain beans and rinse well.
2. Place beans in large saucepan with 4 cups water; bring to a boil. Reduce heat and simmer 1 hour or until beans are tender. Drain beans.
3. Heat oil in large skillet over medium heat. Add onion and garlic; cook and stir 5 minutes or until onion is softened. Add curry powder; cook and stir 30 seconds or until fragrant. Add chard and 2 tablespoons water; cook 5 minutes or until wilted.
4. Add beans to chard mixture; cook and stir until heated through. Stir in remaining ½ teaspoon salt and pepper.

Fruited Curry Chicken Salad Sandwiches

Makes 10 sandwiches (about 7½ cups salad)

- 1 rotisserie chicken
- 1¼ cups halved seedless red grapes
- ½ cup diced Granny Smith apple
- ½ cup sliced almonds, toasted
- ⅓ cup golden raisins
- ⅓ cup dried cranberries
- 1 stalk celery, diced
- ¼ cup unsweetened shredded coconut
- ¼ cup finely diced red onion
- ¾ cup mayonnaise
- 1 tablespoon curry powder
- 1 tablespoon lime juice
- 2 teaspoons honey
- Salt and black pepper
- 10 croissants
- 10 lettuce leaves
- 20 slices tomato

1. Remove skin and bones from chicken; chop meat. Combine chicken, grapes, apple, almonds, raisins, cranberries, celery, coconut and onion in large bowl.
2. Combine mayonnaise, curry powder, lime juice and honey in medium bowl. Add to chicken mixture; stir until well blended. Season to taste with salt and pepper.
3. Cut croissants in half horizontally. Line bottom halves of croissants with lettuce leaves; top with about ¾ cup chicken salad and two tomato slices. Cover with top halves of croissants.

Curried Eggs and Potatoes

Makes 6 servings

- 1 pound yellow potatoes, sliced
- 1 tablespoon vegetable oil
- 1 onion, chopped
- 2 cloves garlic, minced
- 1 piece (1-inch) fresh ginger, peeled and chopped
- 1 tablespoon curry powder
- 1 tablespoon all-purpose flour
- 1 tablespoon mango chutney, plus additional for serving
- 1½ cups vegetable broth
- ½ teaspoon salt
- ⅛ teaspoon black pepper
- 1 package (10 ounces) frozen peas, thawed
- 6 hard-cooked eggs, peeled and quartered
- 6 cups hot cooked rice

1. Cook potatoes in medium saucepan of salted boiling water 5 to 7 minutes or until fork-tender. Drain and return to saucepan; keep warm.
2. Heat oil in large skillet over medium-low heat. Add onion, garlic and ginger; cook and stir 5 minutes or until onion is softened. Add curry powder; cook and stir 30 seconds or until fragrant. *Do not burn.* Stir in flour and 1 tablespoon chutney. Add broth, salt and pepper; cook and stir until sauce is thickened.
3. Add potatoes, peas and eggs; cook until heated through, stirring occasionally. Serve with rice and additional mango chutney, if desired.

Tuna Salad on Toast

Makes 4 servings

- 2 cans (6 ounces each) tuna packed in water, drained
- 3 tablespoons mayonnaise
- 2 tablespoons sour cream or plain yogurt
- 1 tablespoon sugar
- 1 teaspoon curry powder
- ¼ teaspoon ground cumin
- 4 ounces sliced water chestnuts, drained and coarsely chopped
- ⅛ teaspoon ground red pepper
- 4 slices cinnamon-raisin bread, toasted

1. Combine tuna, mayonnaise, sour cream, sugar, curry powder and cumin in medium bowl; mix well. Add water chestnuts and red pepper; mix well. Cover and refrigerate 15 minutes to allow flavors to develop.
2. Serve tuna salad on toast.

Curried Carrots

Makes 4 servings

- 2 teaspoons butter
- 1 tablespoon packed dark brown sugar
- 1 teaspoon curry powder
- ¼ teaspoon ground cumin
- 1 pound carrots, peeled and sliced ⅛ inch thick (about 3 cups)
- ¼ teaspoon salt
- ⅛ teaspoon black pepper
- ¾ cup water
- 2 tablespoons minced fresh parsley

1 Melt butter in large nonstick skillet over medium heat. Add brown sugar, curry powder and cumin; cook and stir 1 minute. Add carrots, salt, pepper and water; cover and bring to a boil. Reduce heat to low. Cook 7 minutes or until carrots are tender.

2 Uncover; cook and stir 5 minutes or until liquid is reduced to about 2 tablespoons. Sprinkle with parsley.

Nutty Veggie Burgers

Makes 4 servings

- 2 eggs
- ⅓ cup plain yogurt
- 2 teaspoons vegetarian Worcestershire sauce or sauce soy
- 2 teaspoons curry powder
- ½ teaspoon salt
- ¼ teaspoon ground red pepper
- 1⅓ cups cooked couscous or brown rice
- ½ cup finely chopped walnuts
- ½ cup grated carrots
- ½ cup minced green onions
- ⅓ cup plain dry bread crumbs
- 4 sesame seed hamburger buns

1. Spray grill grate with nonstick cooking spray. Prepare grill for direct cooking.
2. Combine eggs, yogurt, Worcestershire sauce, curry powder, salt and red pepper in large bowl; beat until blended. Stir in couscous, walnuts, carrots, green onions and bread crumbs. Shape into four 1-inch-thick patties.
3. Grill patties over medium-high heat 5 to 6 minutes per side or until well browned and heated through. Serve on buns.

Note

Burgers can also be broiled 4 inches from heat source for 5 to 6 minutes per side or until done.

Lentil Vegetable Stew

Makes 8 servings

- 3 tablespoons vegetable oil
- 1 large onion, chopped
- 1 can (28 ounces) crushed tomatoes
- 2 cups water
- 1 tablespoon curry powder
- 1 tablespoon cider vinegar
- 1½ teaspoons salt
- 1½ teaspoons ground cumin
- 1½ teaspoons ground coriander
- 1 teaspoon ground ginger
- 1¼ cups dried lentils
- 2 cups cauliflower florets
- 1 cup chopped red bell pepper
- 1 cup chopped yellow squash

1 Heat oil in large saucepan over medium heat. Add onion; cook and stir 5 minutes or until softened. Stir in tomatoes, water, curry powder, vinegar, salt, cumin, coriander and ginger. Stir in lentils; bring to a boil. Reduce heat to medium-low; simmer 35 to 40 minutes or until lentils begin to soften.

2 Add cauliflower, bell pepper and squash; cook 30 to 40 minutes or until vegetables and lentils are tender.

Indian-Style Lamb and Chickpeas

Makes 6 to 8 servings

- 2 tablespoons butter, divided
- 1 onion, chopped
- 3 cloves garlic, chopped
- 2 teaspoons finely chopped fresh ginger
- 1 pound ground lamb
- Salt and black pepper
- 1 pound fresh tomatoes (about 3 medium), diced
- 1 tablespoon curry powder
- ½ teaspoon ground red pepper
- ⅛ teaspoon ground cinnamon
- ⅛ teaspoon ground nutmeg
- 2 cans (about 15 ounces each) chickpeas, rinsed and drained
- ¾ cup plain yogurt
- ½ cup dry bread crumbs

1. Preheat oven to 350°F.
2. Melt 1 tablespoon butter in large skillet over medium-high heat. Add onion, garlic and ginger; cook and stir 2 minutes or until onion begins to soften. Add lamb; cook 6 to 8 minutes or until no longer pink, stirring to break up meat. Season with salt and black pepper.
3. Add tomatoes, curry powder, red pepper, cinnamon and nutmeg; cook and stir 5 minutes. Remove from heat. Add chickpeas and yogurt; stir to combine.
4. Transfer mixture to 2½-quart baking dish. Sprinkle bread crumbs on top and dot with remaining 1 tablespoon butter. Bake 30 minutes or until bubbly and lightly browned.

Red Lentil and Chickpea Stew

Makes 6 servings

- 1 tablespoon olive oil
- 1 onion, chopped
- 2 tablespoons minced fresh ginger
- 3 cloves garlic, minced
- 1 tablespoon curry powder
- 2 teaspoons ground turmeric
- 1½ teaspoons salt
- ⅛ teaspoon ground red pepper
- 4 cups vegetable broth
- 1¼ cups dried red lentils (8 ounces)
- 1 can (about 15 ounces) chickpeas, rinsed and drained
- 1 can (about 14 ounces) coconut milk
- 1 package (about 5 ounces) baby spinach
- Large coconut flakes and chopped fresh cilantro (optional)

1 Heat oil in large saucepan over medium-high heat. Add onion; cook and stir 5 minutes or until softened. Add ginger, garlic, curry powder, turmeric, salt and red pepper; cook and stir 1 minute. Add broth; bring to a boil. Stir in lentils; cook 15 minutes.

2 Stir in chickpeas and coconut milk; cook 5 to 10 minutes or until lentils are tender, chickpeas are heated through and stew is slightly thickened. Add spinach; cook and stir 2 to 3 minutes or just until spinach is wilted. Garnish with coconut and cilantro.

Hot and Sweet Deviled Eggs

Makes 12 deviled eggs

- 6 hard-cooked eggs, peeled and cut in half lengthwise
- ¼ cup mayonnaise
- ½ teaspoon hot curry powder
- ¼ teaspoon black pepper
- ⅛ teaspoon salt
- Dash of paprika
- ¼ cup dried sweetened cherries or cranberries, finely chopped
- 1 teaspoon minced fresh chives, plus additional for garnish

1. Scoop egg yolks into medium bowl; reserve whites. Add mayonnaise, curry powder, pepper, salt and paprika; mash until well blended. Stir in cherries and 1 teaspoon chives.
2. Pipe or spoon yolk mixture into egg whites. Garnish with additional chives.

Chutney Burgers

Makes 4 servings

- 1 pound ground beef
- ¼ cup mango chutney, chopped
- ¼ cup grated apple
- 1½ teaspoons curry powder
- ½ teaspoon salt
- ⅛ teaspoon black pepper
- 1 large red onion, cut into ¼-inch slices
- Lettuce leaves
- 1 large tomato, sliced
- 4 hamburger buns

1. Prepare grill for direct cooking.
2. Combine beef, chutney, apple, curry powder, salt and pepper in medium bowl; mix gently but thoroughly. Shape into four patties.
3. Place patties on grid. Grill, covered, over medium heat 8 to 10 minutes (or uncovered 13 to 15 minutes) or until cooked through (160°F), turning once.
4. Grill onion 5 minutes or until lightly charred, turning once. Place lettuce on bottoms of buns. Top with burgers, tomato, onion and tops of buns.

Ginger

Ginger Beef and Carrot Kabobs

Makes 4 servings

- 12 ounces boneless beef top sirloin steak (1 inch thick), cut into 1-inch cubes
- ¼ cup soy sauce
- 1 tablespoon grated fresh ginger
- 1 tablespoon water
- 1 tablespoon honey
- 1 teaspoon olive oil
- ¼ teaspoon ground allspice
- ⅛ teaspoon ground red pepper
- 1 clove garlic, minced
- 2 medium carrots, cut into 1-inch pieces (1½ cups)
- 4 green onions, trimmed to 4-inch pieces

1 Place beef in large bowl. Combine soy sauce, ginger, water, honey, oil, allspice, red pepper and garlic in small bowl; pour over beef and stir to coat. Cover and marinate in refrigerator 4 to 16 hours, stirring occasionally.

2 Meanwhile, bring 1 inch of water to a boil in medium saucepan over high heat. Add carrots; cover and cook 5 minutes or until crisp-tender. Drain.

3 Spray grill grate with nonstick cooking spray. Prepare grill for direct cooking over medium heat. Drain beef; discard marinade. Alternately thread beef and carrot pieces onto four skewers.* Add green onion piece to end of each skewer.

4 Grill kabobs 11 to 14 minutes or until meat is tender, turning once during grilling.

**If using wooden skewers, soak in cool water 20 to 30 minutes to prevent burning.*

Sticky Chicken with Pineapple Rice

Makes 4 servings

- 2 tablespoons vegetable oil
- 1 onion, chopped
- 2 teaspoons minced fresh garlic
- 1 teaspoon ground ginger
- 1 teaspoon five-spice powder
- 1 cup ketchup
- 1 can (12 ounces) cola beverage
- 1 can (20 ounces) pineapple chunks in juice, drained
- ¼ cup soy sauce
- 2 tablespoons white vinegar
- ¼ cup packed brown sugar
- 4 boneless skinless chicken breasts (about 6 ounces each)
- 2 cups uncooked rice
- 1 can (8 ounces) crushed pineapple, drained
- 1 tablespoon chopped fresh parsley

1. Preheat oven to 350°F. Spray 13×9-inch baking dish with nonstick cooking spray.
2. Heat oil in medium saucepan over medium heat. Add onion; cook and stir 5 minutes until soft and translucent. Stir in garlic, ginger and five-spice powder; cook 1 minute. Add ketchup, cola, pineapple chunks, soy sauce, vinegar and brown sugar; bring to a boil over medium-high heat until mixture is slightly syrupy, about 15 minutes.
3. Place chicken in prepared baking dish; top with pineapple mixture. Bake 30 minutes or until chicken is cooked through (165°F) and no longer pink in center, turning every 10 minutes. Remove to cutting board; let stand 5 minutes.
4. Meanwhile, cook rice according to package directions. Stir in crushed pineapple and parsley. Divide rice among four serving plates; top with chicken, pineapple chunks and sauce.

Chicken Stir-Fry with Peas

Makes 4 to 6 servings

- **1 cup chicken broth**
- **2 tablespoons cornstarch**
- **2 tablespoons vegetable oil**
- **8 boneless skinless chicken thighs, cut into 1-inch pieces**
- **2 tablespoons soy sauce**
- **2 tablespoons dry sherry**
- **1 teaspoon ground ginger**
- **1 teaspoon sugar**
- **¼ teaspoon garlic powder**
- **1 package (10 ounces) frozen green peas, thawed**
- **½ small head iceberg lettuce cut into ½-inch slices**
- **Hot cooked rice**
- **Optional toppings: red onion slices, shredded red cabbage and steamed snow peas (optional)**

1. Whisk broth and cornstarch in small bowl until smooth and well blended.
2. Heat oil in wok over high heat. Add chicken; stir-fry 4 minutes or until well browned and no longer pink in center. Reduce heat to low. Stir in soy sauce, sherry, ginger, sugar and garlic powder; cover and cook 5 minutes.
3. Increase heat to high. Stir peas into wok and stir-fry 2 minutes or until heated through.
4. Stir broth mixture until smooth; stir into wok. Stir-fry until sauce boils and thickens. Add lettuce; stir-fry until wilted. Serve stir-fry over rice with desired toppings.

Moroccan Chickpeas

Makes 6 servings

- 1 tablespoon olive oil
- 1 cup chopped onion
- ½ cup sliced red bell pepper
- ½ cup sliced yellow bell pepper
- ½ cup sliced green bell pepper
- 2 cloves garlic, crushed
- 2 cans (about 15 ounces each) chickpeas, rinsed and drained
- 1 can (28 ounces) diced tomatoes
- ¼ cup vegetable broth or water
- 2 tablespoons oil-cured olives, pitted and chopped
- 1 teaspoon ground cumin
- 1 teaspoon ground ginger
- 1 teaspoon ground turmeric
- ½ teaspoon salt
- 1 bay leaf
- 2 tablespoons lemon juice

1. Heat oil in large skillet over medium-high heat. Add onion, bell peppers and garlic; cook and stir 5 minutes or until onion is softened.
2. Add chickpeas, tomatoes, broth, olives, cumin, ginger, turmeric, salt and bay leaf; simmer 5 minutes or until bell peppers are tender. Remove and discard bay leaf. Stir in lemon juice; adjust seasonings.

Jamaican Grilled Sweet Potatoes

Makes 6 servings

- 2 large sweet potatoes or yams (about 1½ pounds)
- 3 tablespoons packed brown sugar
- 3 tablespoons melted butter, divided
- 1 teaspoon ground ginger
- 1 tablespoon chopped fresh cilantro
- 2 teaspoons dark rum
- Salt and black pepper
- Chopped fresh parsley

1. Pierce potatoes in several places with fork. Place on paper towel in microwave. Microwave on HIGH 5 minutes. Let stand 10 minutes. Diagonally slice potatoes into ¾-inch slices.
2. Prepare grill for direct cooking over medium heat. Combine brown sugar, 1 tablespoon melted butter and ginger in small bowl; mix well. Stir in cilantro and rum; set aside. Lightly brush one side of each potato slice with half of remaining melted butter; season with salt and pepper.
3. Grill sweet potato slices, butter side down, covered, 4 to 6 minutes or until grill marked. Brush tops with remaining melted butter. Turn; grill 3 to 5 minutes or until grill marked. Place in serving dish; top with rum sauce and sprinkle with parsley.

Pumpkin Cheesecake with Ginger Crust

Makes 16 servings

- 12 whole honey graham crackers, broken into small pieces
- 3 tablespoons butter, melted
- 1 teaspoon ground ginger
- 3 packages (8 ounces each) cream cheese, softened
- 1 cup sugar
- 4 eggs
- 1 can (15 ounces) pumpkin purée
- ½ cup evaporated milk
- 1 tablespoon vanilla
- 1 teaspoon ground cinnamon
- ½ teaspoon ground nutmeg
- ¼ teaspoon salt
- Whipped cream and additional ground nutmeg (optional)

1. Preheat oven to 350°F. Spray 9-inch springform pan with nonstick cooking spray.
2. Place graham crackers, butter and ginger in food processor; pulse until coarse crumbs form. Gently press crumb mixture onto bottom and ¾-inch up side of pan. Bake 10 minutes or until lightly browned. Cool slightly in pan on wire rack.
3. Beat cream cheese in large bowl with electric mixer at medium-high speed until smooth. Gradually add sugar; beat until fluffy. Add eggs one at a time, beating well after each addition. Add pumpkin, evaporated milk, vanilla, cinnamon, ½ teaspoon nutmeg and salt; beat at medium speed until smooth and well blended. Pour into crust; smooth top.
4. Bake 1 hour and 15 minutes or until top begins to crack and center is almost set. Cool in pan on wire rack 1 hour. Cover and refrigerate until ready to serve.
5. Run thin knife around edge of pan; remove side of pan. Top with whipped cream and additional nutmeg just before serving, if desired.

Ginger Snack Cake

Makes 24 servings

- 2½ cups all-purpose flour
- 1 teaspoon ground cinnamon
- 1 teaspoon baking powder
- ½ teaspoon baking soda
- ½ teaspoon salt
- ½ teaspoon ground ginger
- ¾ cup milk
- ½ cup sour cream
- 1 cup packed brown sugar
- ½ cup (1 stick) butter, softened
- ¼ cup molasses
- 2 eggs
- ⅔ cup raisins
- ⅔ cup chopped pecans
- ½ cup chopped crystallized ginger

1. Preheat oven to 350°F. Spray 13×9-inch baking pan with nonstick cooking spray. Whisk flour, cinnamon, baking powder, baking soda, salt and ground ginger in medium bowl.
2. Combine milk and sour cream in small bowl. Beat brown sugar, butter and molasses in large bowl with electric mixer at medium speed until fluffy. Add eggs; beat well. Add half of flour mixture; beat at low speed. Add milk mixture and remaining flour mixture; beat until combined. Stir in raisins, pecans and crystallized ginger. Spread batter in prepared pan.
3. Bake 30 to 35 minutes or until toothpick inserted into center comes out clean. Cool completely in pan on wire rack.

Ginger Ice Box Cookies

Makes 2½ to 3 dozen cookies

- **3 cups all-purpose flour**
- **2 teaspoons ground ginger**
- **1 teaspoon baking soda**
- **½ teaspoon salt**
- **½ teaspoon Chinese five-spice powder**
- **½ teaspoon ground cloves**
- **¼ teaspoon ground cinnamon**
- **1 cup (2 sticks) butter, softened**
- **1 cup sugar**
- **½ cup molasses**
- **1 egg**
- **½ cup finely chopped crystallized ginger**
- **2 tablespoons grated orange peel**

1. Whisk flour, ground ginger, baking soda, salt, five-spice powder, cloves and cinnamon in medium bowl.
2. Beat butter and sugar in large bowl with electric mixer at medium speed until creamy. Add molasses and egg; beat until light and fluffy. Gradually beat in flour mixture until well blended. Add crystallized ginger and orange peel; beat until blended.
3. Turn out dough onto sheet of plastic wrap; pat dough into 8×5-inch rectangle, about 1 inch thick. Wrap in plastic wrap; refrigerate about 4 hours or until firm.
4. Preheat oven to 350°F. Line cookie sheets with parchment paper. Cut dough into ¼-inch-thick slices. Place 2 inches apart on prepared cookie sheets.
5. Bake 12 to 14 minutes until deep golden brown. Cool on cookie sheets 5 minutes. Remove to wire racks; cool completely.

Ginger Pear Cobbler

Makes 8 to 10 servings

- 7 firm ripe red pears (about 3½ pounds), peeled and cut into ½-inch pieces
- ⅓ cup packed brown sugar
- 1 cup plus 2 tablespoons all-purpose flour, divided
- 2 tablespoons lemon juice
- 2 teaspoons ground ginger, divided
- ½ teaspoon ground cinnamon
- ⅛ teaspoon ground nutmeg
- ¼ cup granulated sugar
- 1½ teaspoons baking powder
- ¼ teaspoon salt
- ¼ cup (½ stick) cold butter, cut into small pieces
- ¼ cup whipping cream
- 1 egg, lightly beaten
- Sparkling or coarse sugar (optional)

1. Preheat oven to 375°F. Spray 9-inch square baking dish with nonstick cooking spray.
2. Combine pears, brown sugar, 2 tablespoons flour, lemon juice, 1 teaspoon ginger, cinnamon and nutmeg in large bowl; toss to coat. Spoon into prepared baking dish.
3. Whisk remaining 1 cup flour, 1 teaspoon ginger, granulated sugar, baking powder and salt in medium bowl. Add butter; mix with fingertips until shaggy clumps form. Add cream and egg; stir just until combined. Drop topping by 2 tablespoonfuls into mounds over pear mixture. Sprinkle with sparkling sugar, if desired.
4. Bake 40 to 45 minutes or until filling is bubbly and topping is golden brown.

Spiced Pumpkin Muffins

Makes 12 muffins

- 2 cups all-purpose flour
- 2 teaspoons baking powder
- 1 teaspoon baking soda
- 1 teaspoon salt
- 1 teaspoon ground ginger
- ½ teaspoon ground cinnamon
- ½ teaspoon ground nutmeg
- ¼ teaspoon ground cloves
- 1 cup packed brown sugar
- ¾ cup canned pumpkin
- 2 eggs
- ½ cup vegetable oil
- ½ cup slivered almonds, toasted*
- 1 cup powdered sugar
- 2 to 3 tablespoons orange or lemon juice

***To toast almonds, spread on baking sheet. Bake in 350°F oven 5 to 7 minutes or until golden brown, stirring occasionally. Immediately remove from pan; cool before using.**

1. Preheat oven to 350°F. Spray 12 standard (2½-inch) muffin cups with nonstick cooking spray or line with paper baking cups.
2. Whisk flour, baking powder, baking soda, salt, ginger, cinnamon, nutmeg and cloves in medium bowl. Combine brown sugar, pumpkin, eggs and oil in large bowl; beat until well blended. Add flour mixture; stir just until dry ingredients are moistened. Stir in almonds. Spoon batter evenly into prepared muffin cups.
3. Bake 18 to 20 minutes or until toothpick inserted into centers comes out clean. Cool in pan 5 minutes. Remove to wire rack; cool completely.
4. Place powdered sugar in small bowl. Add 2 tablespoons orange juice; whisk until smooth. Add additional juice if necessary to reach drizzling consistency. Drizzle glaze over muffins; let stand until set.

Chocolate Gingerbread Brownies

Makes 16 brownies

Brownies

- ¾ cup all-purpose flour
- ½ cup unsweetened cocoa powder
- 2 teaspoons ground ginger
- 1 teaspoon ground cinnamon
- ½ teaspoon baking powder
- ½ teaspoon salt
- ⅛ teaspoon ground allspice
- ⅛ teaspoon ground cloves
- ⅛ teaspoon ground nutmeg
- ¾ cup packed brown sugar
- ¾ cup granulated sugar
- ¾ cup (1½ sticks) butter, melted and cooled
- 3 eggs
- 2 tablespoons molasses
- 1 teaspoon vanilla

Frosting

- ¼ cup (½ stick) butter, melted
- ¼ cup buttermilk
- ½ teaspoon vanilla
- 2 cups powdered sugar
- 2 tablespoons unsweetened cocoa powder
- 1 teaspoon ground ginger
- ½ teaspoon ground cinnamon

1. Preheat oven to 350°F. Spray 8-inch square baking pan with nonstick cooking spray or line with parchment paper.
2. Whisk flour, ½ cup cocoa, 2 teaspoons ginger, 1 teaspoon cinnamon, baking powder, salt, allspice, cloves and nutmeg in large bowl. Whisk brown sugar, granulated sugar, ¾ cup butter, eggs, molasses and 1 teaspoon vanilla in medium bowl until well blended. Add to flour mixture; mix just until blended. Spread batter into prepared pan.
3. Bake 35 to 40 minutes or until toothpick inserted into center comes out clean. Cool completely in pan on wire rack.
4. For frosting, whisk ¼ cup butter, buttermilk and ½ teaspoon vanilla in small bowl. Add powdered sugar, 2 tablespoons cocoa, 1 teaspoon ginger and ½ teaspoon cinnamon; whisk until smooth. Spread evenly over brownies. Let stand until set.

Cinnamon

Greek Braised Cinnamon Chicken

Makes 4 servings

- 4 chicken leg quarters (drumstick and thigh, 8 to 10 ounces each)
- 1¾ teaspoons salt, divided
- ¾ teaspoon black pepper, divided
- ¼ teaspoon plus ⅛ teaspoon ground cinnamon, divided
- 2 tablespoons olive oil
- 2 medium onions, chopped
- 3 cloves garlic, minced
- 1 can (28 ounces) whole tomatoes, undrained, coarsely chopped or crushed with hands
- ½ cup chicken broth
- 1 cinnamon stick
- Chopped fresh parsley
- Grated Kasseri* or Romano cheese (optional)

**Kasseri is a semi-hard Greek sheep's milk cheese with a mild buttery and slightly piquant flavor.*

1. Preheat oven to 375°F.
2. Season both sides of chicken with ¾ teaspoon salt, ¼ teaspoon pepper and ⅛ teaspoon ground cinnamon. Heat oil in Dutch oven over medium-high heat. Cook chicken in two batches about 5 minutes per side or until browned. Remove to plate. Drain off all but 2 tablespoons fat.
3. Add onions to Dutch oven; cook and stir 5 minutes or until softened, scraping up browned bits from bottom of pot. Add garlic and remaining ¼ teaspoon ground cinnamon; cook and stir 1 minute. Stir in tomatoes with liquid, broth, cinnamon stick, remaining 1 teaspoon salt and ½ teaspoon pepper; mix well. Return chicken to Dutch oven, skin side up, pressing down to partially submerge chicken in sauce.
4. Cover and bake 40 minutes. Remove cover; bake 15 minutes or until chicken is cooked through (165°F). Serve with parsley and cheese, if desired.

Warm Apple Crostata

Makes 4 tarts (4 to 8 servings)

- 1¾ cups all-purpose flour
- ⅓ cup granulated sugar
- ½ teaspoon plus ⅛ teaspoon salt, divided
- ¾ cup (1½ sticks) cold butter, cut into small pieces
- 3 tablespoons ice water
- 2 teaspoons vanilla
- 4 Pink Lady or Honeycrisp apples (about 1½ pounds), peeled and cut into ¼-inch slices
- ¼ cup packed brown sugar
- 1 tablespoon lemon juice
- 1 teaspoon ground cinnamon
- ⅛ teaspoon ground nutmeg
- 4 teaspoons butter, cut into very small pieces
- 1 egg, beaten
- 1 to 2 teaspoons coarse sugar
- Vanilla ice cream
- Caramel sauce or ice cream topping

1. Combine flour, granulated sugar and ½ teaspoon salt in food processor; process 5 seconds. Add ¾ cup cold butter; process 10 seconds or until mixture resembles coarse crumbs.
2. Combine ice water and vanilla in small bowl. With motor running, pour mixture through feed tube; process 12 seconds or until dough begins to come together. Shape dough into a disc; wrap with plastic wrap and refrigerate 30 minutes.
3. Meanwhile, combine apples, brown sugar, lemon juice, cinnamon, nutmeg and remaining ⅛ teaspoon salt in large bowl; toss to coat. Preheat oven to 400°F.
4. Line two large baking sheets with parchment paper. Cut dough into four pieces; roll out each piece into 7-inch circle on floured surface. Place on prepared baking sheets; mound apples in center of dough circles (about 1 cup apples for each crostata). Fold or roll up edges of dough towards center to create rim of crostata. Dot apples with 4 teaspoons butter. Brush dough with egg; sprinkle dough and apples with coarse sugar.
5. Bake 20 minutes or until apples are tender and crust is golden brown. Serve warm topped with ice cream and caramel sauce.

Iced Cinnamon Buns

Makes 12 buns

Dough

- 1 package (¼ ounce) active dry yeast
- 1 cup warm milk (110°F)
- 2 eggs, beaten
- ½ cup granulated sugar
- ¼ cup (½ stick) butter, softened
- 1 teaspoon salt
- 4 to 4¼ cups all-purpose flour

Filling

- 1 cup packed brown sugar
- 3 tablespoons ground cinnamon
- Pinch salt
- 6 tablespoons butter, softened

Icing

- 1½ cups powdered sugar
- 3 ounces cream cheese, softened
- ¼ cup (½ stick) butter, softened
- ½ teaspoon vanilla
- ⅛ teaspoon salt

1. Dissolve yeast in warm milk in large bowl of electric stand mixer. Add eggs, granulated sugar, ¼ cup butter and 1 teaspoon salt; beat at medium speed until well blended. Add 4 cups flour; beat at low speed until dough begins to come together. Knead dough with dough hook at low speed 5 minutes or until dough is smooth, elastic and slightly sticky. Add additional flour, 1 tablespoon at a time, if necessary to prevent sticking.

2. Shape dough into a ball. Place in large greased bowl; turn to grease top. Cover and let rise in warm place 1 hour or until doubled in size. Meanwhile for filling, combine brown sugar, cinnamon and pinch of salt in small bowl.

3. Spray 13×9-inch baking pan with nonstick cooking spray. Roll out dough into 18×14-inch rectangle on floured surface. Spread 6 tablespoons butter evenly over dough; top with cinnamon-sugar mixture. Beginning with long side, roll up dough tightly jelly-roll style; pinch seam to seal. Cut log crosswise into 12 slices; place slices cut sides up in prepared pan. Cover and let rise in warm place 30 minutes or until almost doubled in size. Preheat oven to 350°F.

4. Bake 20 to 25 minutes or until golden brown. Meanwhile for icing, combine powdered sugar, cream cheese, ¼ cup butter, vanilla and ⅛ teaspoon salt in medium bowl; beat with electric mixer at medium speed 2 minutes or until smooth and creamy. Spread icing generously over warm cinnamon buns.

Tropical Bread Pudding with Orange Sauce

Makes 10 to 12 servings

- ¾ cup raisins
- 3 cups milk
- 3 eggs
- 1 cup sugar
- 1 cup shredded coconut
- ⅔ cup coarsely chopped walnuts
- 3 tablespoons butter, melted
- 2 tablespoons vanilla
- 1 teaspoon ground nutmeg
- ½ teaspoon ground cinnamon
- 1 jar (8 ounces) maraschino cherries, undrained
- 1 can (11 ounces) mandarin orange segments, undrained
- 1 loaf (16 ounces) cinnamon-raisin bread, torn into 2-inch pieces
- Orange Sauce (recipe follows, optional)

1. Preheat oven to 350°F. Spray 13×9-inch baking pan with nonstick cooking spray.
2. Place raisins in small bowl. Pour boiling water over to cover. Let stand 2 to 3 minutes or until plump. Drain.
3. Combine raisins, milk, eggs, sugar, coconut, walnuts, butter, vanilla, nutmeg and cinnamon in large bowl; mix well. Add cherries and oranges with liquid; mix well.
4. Add bread pieces to milk mixture. Pour into prepared pan.
5. Bake 1 hour to 1 hour and 15 minutes or until knife inserted near center comes out clean. Meanwhile, prepare Orange Sauce. Serve warm with bread pudding.

Orange Sauce

Combine 1½ cups powdered sugar, ½ cup (1 stick) butter and ¼ cup whipping cream in medium saucepan; whisk in 1 egg yolk. Cook over medium heat until thickened, stirring constantly. Remove from heat; stir in 2 tablespoons orange liqueur.

Cappuccino Crunch Bars

Makes about 2½ dozen bars

- 1¾ cups all-purpose flour, sifted
- 1 teaspoon baking soda
- 1 teaspoon salt
- ½ teaspoon ground cinnamon
- 1½ cups packed brown sugar
- 1 cup (2 sticks) butter, softened
- ½ cup granulated sugar
- 2 eggs
- 2 teaspoons instant coffee granules or espresso powder, dissolved in 1 tablespoon hot water
- 2 teaspoons vanilla
- 1 teaspoon grated orange peel (optional)
- 1 cup white chocolate chips
- 1 cup chocolate-covered toffee baking bits

1. Preheat oven to 350°F. Spray 13×9-inch baking pan with nonstick cooking spray or line with parchment paper. Whisk flour, baking soda, salt and cinnamon in medium bowl.

2. Beat brown sugar, butter and granulated sugar in large bowl with electric mixer at medium speed until fluffy. Add eggs, one at a time, beating well after each addition. Add coffee mixture, vanilla and orange peel, if desired; beat well. Gradually add flour mixture at low speed, beating just until well blended. Stir in white chocolate chips and toffee bits. Spread batter evenly in prepared pan.

3. Bake 25 to 35 minutes or until golden brown and center is firm to the touch. Cool completely in pan on wire rack. Cut into bars.

Cinnamon Scones

Makes 12 scones

- **2 cups all-purpose flour**
- **¼ cup plus 2 tablespoons sugar, divided**
- **2½ teaspoons baking powder**
- **¾ teaspoon salt**
- **½ teaspoon baking soda**
- **½ cup (1 stick) cold butter, cut into small pieces**
- **⅓ cup cinnamon chips**
- **¾ cup whipping cream or whole milk**
- **½ cup plain yogurt or sour cream**
- **1½ teaspoons ground cinnamon**

1. Preheat oven to 425°F.
2. Combine flour, ¼ cup sugar, baking powder, salt and baking soda in large bowl. Cut in butter with pastry blender or fingertips until coarse crumbs form. Add cinnamon chips; toss to combine.
3. Whisk cream and yogurt in small bowl until combined. Stir into flour mixture just until dough begins to form. Turn out dough onto floured surface. Knead 5 or 6 times until dough holds together.
4. Divide dough into two pieces. Pat each piece into 5-inch circle, about ½ inch thick. Cut each circle into six wedges using floured knife. Place scones 2 inches apart on large baking sheet. Combine remaining 2 tablespoons sugar and cinnamon in small bowl; sprinkle over scones.
5. Bake 10 to 14 minutes or until lightly browned. Remove to wire rack; serve warm or cool completely.

Loaded Oatmeal Cookies

Makes about 3 dozen cookies

- 1½ cups old-fashioned oats
- 1 cup all-purpose flour
- ½ teaspoon baking soda
- ½ teaspoon salt
- ½ teaspoon ground cinnamon
- 1 cup packed brown sugar
- ¾ cup (1½ sticks) butter, softened
- 1 egg
- 1 tablespoon milk
- 1 teaspoon vanilla
- 1 cup semisweet chocolate chips
- 1 cup butterscotch chips
- ¾ cup raisins
- ½ cup chopped walnuts

1. Preheat oven to 350°F. Combine oats, flour, baking soda, salt and cinnamon in medium bowl.
2. Beat brown sugar and butter in large bowl with electric mixer at medium speed until creamy. Add egg, milk and vanilla; beat until light and fluffy. Gradually add oat mixture at low speed, beating just until blended. Stir in chips, raisins and walnuts.
3. Drop dough by rounded tablespoonfuls 2 inches apart onto ungreased cookie sheets.
4. Bake 12 to 15 minutes or until edges are lightly browned. Cool on cookie sheets 2 minutes. Remove to wire racks; cool completely.

Apple Butter Spice Muffins

Makes 12 muffins

- ½ cup sugar
- 1 teaspoon ground cinnamon
- ¼ teaspoon ground nutmeg
- ⅛ teaspoon ground allspice
- ½ cup chopped pecans or walnuts
- 2 cups all-purpose flour
- 2 teaspoons baking powder
- ¼ teaspoon salt
- 1 cup milk
- ¼ cup vegetable oil
- 1 egg
- ¼ cup apple butter

1. Preheat oven to 400°F. Line 12 standard (2½-inch) muffin cups with paper baking cups or spray with nonstick cooking spray.
2. Combine sugar, cinnamon, nutmeg and allspice in large bowl; remove 2 tablespoons sugar mixture to small bowl. Add pecans to small bowl; toss until coated. Add flour, baking powder and salt to remaining sugar mixture in large bowl.
3. Whisk milk, oil and egg in medium bowl until well blended. Add to flour mixture; stir just until dry ingredients are moistened. Spoon 1 tablespoon batter into each prepared muffin cup. Top with 1 teaspoon apple butter; spoon remaining batter evenly over apple butter. Sprinkle with pecan mixture.
4. Bake 18 to 20 minutes or until golden brown and toothpick inserted into centers comes out clean. Cool in pan 5 minutes. Remove to wire rack; serve warm or cool completely.

Cinnamon Ginger Pumpkin Pie

Makes 8 servings

- 1 refrigerated pie crust (half of 14-ounce package)
- 1 tablespoon sugar
- 1 tablespoon ground cinnamon
- 2 teaspoons ground ginger
- 1 teaspoon ground cloves
- 1 teaspoon ground nutmeg
- ½ teaspoon salt
- 3 eggs
- 2½ teaspoons vanilla
- 1 can (15 ounces) pumpkin purée
- ⅓ cup sour cream
- 1 can (14 ounces) sweetened condensed milk
- Whole pecans (optional)
- Sweetened whipped cream (optional)

1. Preheat oven to 425°F. Line 9-inch deep dish pie plate with pie crust; flute edges.
2. Combine sugar, cinnamon, ginger, cloves, nutmeg and salt in large bowl; mix well. Whisk in eggs and vanilla until smooth. Add pumpkin and sour cream; whisk until smooth. Gradually stir in sweetened condensed milk; whisk until well blended. Pour into crust.
3. Bake 15 minutes. *Reduce oven temperature to 350°F.* Bake 40 to 45 minutes or until knife inserted near center comes out clean. Cool on wire rack at least 1½ hours before serving. Garnish with pecans and whipped cream.

Strawberry-Rhubarb Crisp

Makes 8 servings

- 4 cups sliced rhubarb (1-inch pieces)
- 3 cups sliced fresh strawberries (about 1 pint)
- ¾ cup granulated sugar
- ⅓ cup plus ¼ cup all-purpose flour, divided
- 1 tablespoon grated lemon peel
- 1 cup quick oats
- ½ cup packed brown sugar
- 1 teaspoon ground cinnamon
- ½ teaspoon salt
- ⅓ cup butter, melted

1. Preheat oven to 375°F.
2. Combine rhubarb and strawberries in large bowl. Add granulated sugar, ¼ cup flour and lemon peel; toss to coat. Spread in 9-inch square baking pan.
3. Combine oats, brown sugar, remaining ⅓ cup flour, cinnamon and salt in medium bowl. Stir in butter until crumbly. Sprinkle over fruit mixture.
4. Bake 45 to 50 minutes or until filling is bubbly and topping is lightly browned. Serve warm or at room temperature.

Spice Brownies

Makes 3 dozen brownies

- 1¼ cups all-purpose flour
- ⅔ cup unsweetened cocoa powder
- 1 teaspoon baking powder
- 1 teaspoon salt
- 1 teaspoon ground cinnamon
- 2 cups sugar
- 4 eggs
- ¾ cup (1½ sticks) butter, melted and cooled
- ¾ cup chopped macadamia nuts
- ¼ cup finely chopped crystallized ginger

1. Preheat oven to 350°F. Spray 13×9-inch baking pan with nonstick cooking spray. Whisk flour, cocoa, baking powder, salt and cinnamon in medium bowl.
2. Combine sugar, eggs and butter in large bowl; whisk until well blended. Add flour mixture, nuts and ginger; stir until blended. Spread batter in prepared pan.
3. Bake 25 to 30 minutes or until toothpick inserted into center comes out clean. Cool completely in pan on wire rack.

Chipotle

Southwestern BLT

Makes 2 servings

- 6 slices thick-cut applewood smoked bacon
- ¼ cup mayonnaise
- 1 teaspoon lime juice
- ¼ teaspoon chipotle chili powder
- ¼ teaspoon ground cumin
- 1 large ripe tomato
- 2 pretzel rolls, split and toasted
- ½ cup shredded lettuce

1. Cook bacon in large skillet over medium heat; drain on paper towel-lined plate.
2. Combine mayonnaise, lime juice, chipotle chili powder and cumin in small bowl; mix well.
3. Cut tomato into four thick slices. Spread cut sides of rolls with mayonnaise mixture. Top bottom halves of rolls with lettuce, tomato, bacon and top halves of rolls.

Cauliflower and Mushroom Tacos with Chipotle Crema

Makes 8 tacos

- 1 package (8 ounces) sliced cremini mushrooms
- 4 tablespoons olive oil, divided
- 1¾ teaspoons salt, divided
- 1 head cauliflower, cut into florets
- 1 teaspoon ground cumin
- ½ teaspoon dried oregano
- ¼ teaspoon ground coriander
- ¼ teaspoon ground cinnamon
- ¼ teaspoon black pepper
- ½ cup sour cream
- 2 teaspoons lime juice
- ½ teaspoon chipotle chili powder
- ½ cup vegetarian refried beans
- 8 taco-size flour or corn tortillas
- Sliced red onion or Pickled Red Onions (recipe follows)
- Chopped fresh cilantro (optional)

1. Preheat oven to 400°F. Toss mushrooms with 1 tablespoon oil and ¼ teaspoon salt in large bowl. Spread on small baking sheet.
2. Place cauliflower in same large bowl. Add remaining 3 tablespoons oil, 1 teaspoon salt, cumin, oregano, coriander, cinnamon and black pepper; mix well. Spread on large baking sheet in single layer.
3. Roast cauliflower 40 minutes or until browned and tender, stirring occasionally. Roast mushrooms 20 minutes or until dry and browned, stirring occasionally.
4. For crema, combine sour cream, lime juice, chipotle chili powder and remaining ½ teaspoon salt in small bowl; mix well.
5. For each taco, spread 1 tablespoon beans over tortilla; spread 1 teaspoon crema over beans. Top with about 3 mushroom slices and ¼ cup cauliflower. Top with red onions and cilantro, if desired. Fold in half.

Pickled Red Onions

Thinly slice 1 small red onion; place in large glass jar. Add ¼ cup white wine vinegar or distilled white vinegar, 2 tablespoons water, 1 teaspoon sugar and 1 teaspoon salt. Seal jar; shake well. Refrigerate at least 1 hour or up to 1 week. Makes about ½ cup.

Chipotle Orange BBQ Drumsticks

Makes 8 servings

- ½ cup barbecue sauce, preferably mesquite or hickory smoked
- 1 to 2 tablespoons minced canned chipotle peppers in adobo sauce
- 1 teaspoon grated orange peel
- 8 chicken drumsticks (7 to 8 ounces each), skin removed, rinsed and patted dry
- 1 teaspoon ground cumin
- Salt and black pepper

1. Spray grill grid with nonstick cooking spray. Prepare grill for direct cooking.
2. For sauce, combine barbecue sauce, chipotle peppers and orange peel in small bowl. Set aside.
3. Sprinkle drumsticks evenly with cumin; season all over with salt and black pepper.
4. Grill chicken, covered, over medium-high heat 30 to 35 minutes or until cooked through (165°F), turning frequently. Baste with sauce during last 5 minutes, turning and basting until all of sauce is used.

Cauliflower, Sausage and Gouda Sheet Pan

Makes 6 servings

1 package (16 ounces) mushrooms, trimmed and halved

3 tablespoons olive oil, divided

1 teaspoon salt, divided

1 head cauliflower, separated into florets and thinly sliced

½ teaspoon chipotle chili powder

1 package (about 13 ounces) smoked sausage, cut into ¼-inch slices

2 tablespoons peach or apricot preserves

1 tablespoon Dijon mustard

½ red onion, thinly sliced

6 ounces Gouda cheese, cubed

1. Preheat oven to 400°F.
2. Place mushrooms in medium bowl. Drizzle with 1 tablespoon oil and sprinkle with ½ teaspoon salt; toss to coat. Spread on large baking sheet.
3. Combine cauliflower, remaining 2 tablespoons oil, ½ teaspoon salt and chipotle chili powder in same bowl; toss to coat. Spread on baking sheet with mushrooms.
4. Combine sausage, preserves and mustard in same bowl; stir until well coated. Arrange sausage over vegetables; top with onion.
5. Bake 30 minutes. Remove from oven; place cheese cubes on top of cauliflower. Bake 5 minutes or until cheese is melted and cauliflower is tender.

Hot Cheese-Chipotle Dip

Makes 8 servings (3 cups)

- 2 tablespoons butter
- 1 onion, chopped
- ½ red bell pepper, finely chopped
- 1 clove garlic, minced
- 2 tablespoons all-purpose flour
- 1 can (about 14 ounces) diced tomatoes, 2 tablespoons juice reserved
- 1 cup lager or pilsner beer, preferably Mexican
- 1 canned chipotle pepper in adobo sauce, minced, plus 1 teaspoon adobo sauce
- 4 cups (16 ounces) shredded Mexican-style cheese blend
- Chopped fresh cilantro (optional)
- Tortilla chips

1. Melt butter in medium saucepan over medium heat. Add onion, bell pepper and garlic; cook and stir 5 minutes or until tender. Add flour; stir until well blended. Stir in tomatoes and reserved juice, lager, chipotle pepper and adobo sauce; bring to a boil. Reduce heat to low; simmer 5 minutes or until thickened.
2. Remove from heat. Add cheese blend, 1 cup at a time, stirring until melted after each addition. If necessary, return to very low heat and stir just until melted (do not overcook or the cheese will become gritty). Sprinkle with cilantro, if desired. Serve warm with tortilla chips.

Tip

For a zestier flavor, add more adobo sauce from the canned chipotle.

Chicken Meatballs with Chipotle-Honey Sauce

Makes 48 meatballs

Meatballs

- 2 pounds ground chicken
- 2 eggs, lightly beaten
- ⅓ cup plain dry bread crumbs
- ⅓ cup chopped fresh cilantro
- 2 tablespoons lime juice
- 4 cloves garlic, minced
- 1 can (4 ounces) chipotle peppers in adobo sauce, divided
- 1 teaspoon salt

Chipotle-Honey Sauce

- ¾ cup honey
- 2 to 3 whole chipotle peppers in adobo sauce
- ⅓ cup chicken broth
- ⅓ cup tomato paste
- 1 tablespoon lime juice
- 2 teaspoons Dijon mustard
- ½ teaspoon salt
- 2 tablespoons vegetable oil

1. Line two baking sheets with parchment paper. Combine chicken, eggs, bread crumbs, cilantro, lime juice, garlic, 1 tablespoon adobo sauce and salt in medium bowl; mix well. Shape mixture into 48 meatballs. Place meatballs on prepared baking sheets. Cover with plastic wrap; refrigerate 1 hour.

2. For Chipotle-Honey Sauce, combine honey, chipotle peppers, broth, tomato paste, lime juice, mustard and ½ teaspoon salt in food processor or blender; blend until smooth.

3. Preheat oven to 400°F. Brush meatballs with oil. Bake 12 minutes. Transfer meatballs to baking dish. Add sauce; stir until coated. Bake 10 minutes or until meatballs are heated through and glazed with sauce.

Shredded Chipotle Pork Tacos

Makes 16 tacos

- 6 cups water
- 2 pounds boneless pork shoulder roast, cut into 2-inch, pieces
- 1 medium onion, thinly sliced
- 4 tablespoons cider vinegar, divided
- 1 teaspoon salt
- 1 tablespoon olive oil
- 1 cup finely chopped onion
- 4 cloves garlic, minced
- 1 can (about 8 ounces) tomato sauce
- 3 chipotle peppers in adobo sauce, finely chopped and mashed with a fork
- ½ teaspoon ground cumin
- Roasted Green Onions (recipe follows, optional)
- 16 (6-inch) corn tortillas

1 Combine water, pork, sliced onion, 3 tablespoons vinegar and salt in large saucepan or Dutch oven; bring to a boil over high heat. Reduce heat; simmer, partially covered, 1½ hours or until very tender. Remove pork with slotted spoon to large cutting board and cool slightly; reserve 1 cup cooking liquid. Shred pork with two forks.

2 Heat oil in large nonstick skillet over medium-high heat. Add chopped onion; cook and stir 5 minutes or until softened. Add garlic; cook 15 seconds. Add tomato sauce, chipotle peppers, cumin, remaining 1 tablespoon vinegar, shredded pork and reserved cooking liquid; cook and stir 2 minutes or until heated through. Remove from heat. Cover and let stand 10 minutes.

3 Meanwhile, prepare Roasted Green Onions, if desired. Heat tortillas over stovetop burner or grill about 15 seconds per side or until lightly charred. Fill each tortilla evenly with pork mixture and Roasted Green Onions.

Roasted Green Onions

Preheat oven to 425°F. Trim 16 green onions; place on large baking sheet. Drizzle with 2 teaspoons olive oil; toss gently to coat and arrange in single layer. Bake 10 minutes or until charred. Sprinkle with salt.

Chipotle Lamb Chops with Crispy Potatoes

Makes 2 servings

- 4 lamb loin chops
- 2 teaspoons chipotle chili powder
- Salt and black pepper
- 8 ounces fingerling potatoes
- 3 tablespoons olive oil, divided

1. Rub lamb chops with chipotle chili powder. Season with salt and pepper.
2. Cut potatoes into ¼-inch-thick slices. Heat 2 tablespoons oil in large nonstick skillet over medium heat. Add potatoes, stirring to coat with oil; season with salt and pepper. Cook 15 to 20 minutes or until golden brown and crispy, stirring occasionally.
3. Meanwhile, heat remaining 1 tablespoon oil in medium skillet over medium-high heat. Add lamb chops. Cook 12 to 15 minutes or until medium-rare (145°F), turning once. Serve lamb chops with potatoes.

Chipotle Strip Steaks

Makes 4 servings

- 1 tablespoon olive oil
- ⅓ cup finely chopped onion
- ¾ cup beer
- 1 teaspoon Worcestershire sauce
- ⅓ cup ketchup
- 1 tablespoon red wine vinegar
- 1 teaspoon sugar
- ¼ teaspoon chipotle chili powder
- 4 bone-in strip steaks (about 8 ounces each)
- 1 teaspoon salt

1. Heat oil in small saucepan over medium-high heat. Add onion; cook 3 minutes or until softened, stirring occasionally. Add beer and Worcestershire sauce; bring to a boil, stirring occasionally. Cook until reduced to about ⅓ cup. Stir in ketchup, vinegar, sugar and chipotle chili powder; simmer over medium-low heat 3 minutes or until thickened, stirring occasionally. Keep warm.
2. Spray grill grate with nonstick cooking spray. Prepare grill for direct cooking over medium-high heat. Sprinkle steaks with salt.
3. Grill steaks 4 to 5 minutes per side for medium rare (145°F) or until desired doneness. Serve with chipotle sauce.

Sweet Potato and Turkey Sausage Hash

Makes 2 servings

- 1 mild or hot turkey Italian sausage link (about 4 ounces)
- 1 tablespoon olive oil
- 1 red onion, chopped
- 1 red bell pepper, finely chopped
- 1 small sweet potato, peeled and cut into ½-inch cubes
- ¼ teaspoon salt
- ¼ teaspoon black pepper
- ⅛ teaspoon ground cumin
- ⅛ teaspoon chipotle chili powder

1. Remove sausage from casings; shape sausage into ½-inch balls. Heat oil in large nonstick skillet over medium heat. Add sausage; cook and stir 3 to 5 minutes or until browned. Transfer to plate.
2. Add onion, bell pepper, sweet potato, salt and black pepper, cumin and chipotle chili powder; cook and stir 5 to 8 minutes or until sweet potato is tender.
3. Stir in sausage; cook without stirring 5 minutes or until hash is lightly browned.

Spicy

Baked Buffalo Chicken Dip

Makes about 16 servings (2 cups)

- 1 package (8 ounces) cream cheese, cut into cubes
- ¼ cup crumbled blue cheese
- 2 cups chopped cooked chicken breast (about 8 ounces)
- 3 tablespoons mayonnaise
- 3 tablespoons sour cream
- ¼ to ½ cup hot pepper sauce
- 1 cup (4 ounces) shredded Monterey Jack cheese
- 2 tablespoons panko bread crumbs
- Assorted vegetable sticks and/or pita chips

1. Preheat oven to 400°F. Spray 1-quart baking dish with nonstick cooking spray.
2. Combine cream cheese and blue cheese in medium saucepan; heat over medium heat until melted. Remove from heat. Stir in chicken, mayonnaise, sour cream and hot pepper sauce until combined.
3. Spread chicken mixture in prepared casserole. Sprinkle with Monterey Jack cheese; top evenly with panko. Spray with cooking spray.
4. Bake 20 minutes or until lightly browned and heated through. Serve with assorted vegetable sticks and/or pita chips.

Chicken and Waffles with Sriracha Maple Syrup

Makes 4 to 6 servings

Chicken

- ½ cup milk
- 1 egg
- 1¼ pounds chicken tenderloins (about 8 pieces)
- 1½ cups panko bread crumbs
- 1 teaspoon salt
- 1 teaspoon garlic powder
- 1 teaspoon paprika
- ½ teaspoon black pepper
- ¼ cup vegetable oil

Waffles

- 2 cups pancake and baking mix
- 1⅓ cups milk
- 1 egg

Sriracha Maple Syrup

- ½ cup maple syrup
- 2 teaspoons sriracha hot sauce

1. Whisk ½ cup milk and 1 egg in medium bowl until blended. Add chicken; stir to coat.
2. Combine panko, salt, garlic powder, paprika and pepper in shallow dish. Working with one piece at a time, coat chicken with panko mixture, pressing down lightly to adhere.
3. Heat oil in large skillet over medium-high heat. Reduce heat to medium; cook chicken about 6 minutes per side or until golden brown and no longer pink in center (165°F). Transfer to plate; tent with foil to keep warm.
4. Preheat waffle maker to medium; spray with nonstick cooking spray. Combine baking mix, milk and 1 egg in medium bowl; mix well. Pour ¾ cup batter into waffle maker; cook 3 to 4 minutes or until golden brown. Place on serving plate. Repeat with remaining batter.
5. Combine maple syrup and sriracha in small bowl; mix well. Serve waffles topped with chicken; drizzle with syrup.

Sweet and Spicy Boneless Chicken Wings

Makes 4 to 6 servings

Sauce

- ¾ cup water
- 1 tablespoon cornstarch
- ¼ cup packed dark brown sugar
- ¼ cup soy sauce
- 3 tablespoons lime juice
- 2 tablespoons minced fresh ginger
- 1 teaspoon minced garlic
- ¼ teaspoon red pepper flakes

Chicken

- 2 pounds boneless skinless chicken breasts
- 1 cup all-purpose flour
- ¼ cup cornstarch
- 2 teaspoons salt
- ¼ teaspoon black pepper
- ¼ teaspoon ground red pepper
- ¼ teaspoon sweet paprika
- 2 eggs
- ½ cup milk
- Vegetable oil for frying
- Ranch dressing (optional)

1. For sauce, whisk water and 1 tablespoon cornstarch in medium saucepan until smooth. Add brown sugar, soy sauce, lime juice, ginger, garlic and red pepper flakes; whisk until well blended. Bring to a boil over high heat. Reduce heat to low; simmer 10 minutes or until thickened, stirring occasionally. Pour into large bowl; set aside.
2. Cut chicken into large, wing-shaped pieces (about 2×1 inches). Combine flour, ¼ cup cornstarch, salt, black pepper, ground red pepper and paprika in shallow dish. Beat eggs and milk in another shallow dish. Coat chicken with flour mixture. Dip in egg mixture, letting excess drip back into dish. Coat again with flour mixture; place on large baking sheet.
3. Heat 3 inches of oil in large saucepan or Dutch oven over medium-high heat to 375°F; adjust heat to maintain temperature during cooking. Cook chicken in batches 3 minutes or until golden brown and cooked through (165°F), turning once. Drain on paper towel-lined plate.
4. Add hot cooked chicken to sauce; stir to coat. Transfer to serving plate with slotted spoon. Serve with ranch dressing.

Hot and Spicy Spuds

Makes 4 servings

- 4 medium baking potatoes
- 1 tablespoon olive oil
- 1 cup chopped onion
- ½ cup chopped green bell pepper
- 2 cloves garlic, minced
- 1 can (about 15 ounces) kidney beans, rinsed and drained
- 1 can (about 14 ounces) diced tomatoes
- 1 can (4 ounces) diced mild green chiles
- ¼ cup chopped fresh cilantro or parsley
- 1 teaspoon salt
- 1 teaspoon ground cumin
- 1 teaspoon chili powder
- ¼ teaspoon ground red pepper
- Sour cream
- Shredded Cheddar cheese or queso dip

1. Preheat oven to 350°F. Scrub potatoes; pierce with fork. Place directly on oven rack; bake 1¼ to 1½ hours or until tender.
2. Meanwhile, heat oil in medium saucepan over medium heat. Add onion, bell pepper and garlic; cook and stir 5 minutes or until vegetables are tender. Stir in beans, tomatoes, chiles, cilantro, salt, cumin, chili powder and red pepper. Bring to a boil over high heat. Reduce heat to medium-low; cover and simmer 8 minutes, stirring occasionally.
3. Gently roll potatoes to loosen pulp. Cut crisscross slit in each potato. Place potatoes on four plates; press potato ends to open slits. Spoon bean mixture over potatoes. Serve with sour cream and cheese.

Buffalo Cauliflower Bites

Makes 8 servings

- ¾ cup all-purpose flour
- ¼ cup cornstarch
- 1 teaspoon salt
- ½ teaspoon garlic powder
- ¼ teaspoon black pepper
- 1 cup water
- 1 large head cauliflower (2½ pounds), cut into 1-inch florets
- ½ cup hot pepper sauce
- ¼ cup (½ stick) butter, melted
- Blue cheese or ranch dressing and celery sticks for serving

1. Preheat oven to 450°F. Line baking sheet with foil; spray foil with nonstick cooking spray.
2. Whisk flour, cornstarch, salt, garlic powder and black pepper in large bowl. Whisk in water until smooth and well blended. Add cauliflower to batter in batches; stir to coat. Arrange on prepared baking sheet.
3. Bake 20 minutes or until cauliflower is lightly browned.
4. Meanwhile, combine hot pepper sauce and butter in small bowl; mix well. Pour over hot cauliflower; toss to coat. Bake 5 to 10 minutes or until cauliflower is glazed and crisp, stirring occasionally. Serve with blue cheese dressing and celery sticks.

Hot Chicken Sandwich

Makes 4 to 6 servings

- 2 tablespoons hot pepper sauce, divided
- 2 tablespoons dill pickle juice, divided
- 1 teaspoon salt, divided
- 2 pounds chicken strips or tenders
- 1 cup all-purpose flour
- ½ teaspoon black pepper
- 1 egg
- ½ cup buttermilk
- Vegetable oil for frying
- ¼ cup olive oil
- 1 tablespoon red pepper flakes
- 1 tablespoon packed brown sugar
- ½ teaspoon sweet paprika
- ½ teaspoon chili powder
- ¼ teaspoon garlic powder
- 4 to 6 Brioche buns, toasted
- White Cheddar cheese slices (optional)
- Cole slaw and dill pickle slices (optional)

1. Combine 1 tablespoon hot sauce, 1 tablespoon pickle juice and ½ teaspoon salt in large resealable plastic bag. Add chicken; seal and turn to coat. Refrigerate 1 hour or overnight.

2. Combine flour, remaining ½ teaspoon salt and black pepper in shallow dish. Whisk egg, buttermilk, remaining 1 tablespoon hot sauce and remaining 1 tablespoon pickle juice in another shallow dish. Remove chicken from marinade; discard marinade. Coat chicken with flour mixture, then dip in egg mixture and again in flour mixture.

3. Heat 2 inches of vegetable oil in large saucepan or Dutch oven over medium-high heat to 360° to 370°F; adjust heat to maintain temperature during cooking. Working in batches, add chicken; cook 5 minutes or until cooked through (165°F). Transfer chicken to paper towel-lined plate.

4. Meanwhile, combine olive oil, red pepper flakes, brown sugar, paprika, chili powder and garlic powder in large bowl. Add chicken; toss to coat. Serve chicken on buns with cheese, cole slaw and pickles.

Taco Casserole

Makes 4 to 6 servings

- 2 pounds ground beef
- 1 can (10 ounces) diced tomatoes with mild green chiles
- 1 teaspoon salt
- 1 teaspoon garlic powder
- 1 teaspoon ground cumin
- 1 teaspoon sweet paprika
- 1 teaspoon chili powder
- ½ teaspoon ground red pepper
- ½ teaspoon red pepper flakes
- 1 bag (12 ounces) nacho-cheese flavored tortilla chips, crushed
- ½ cup chopped green onions
- 1 cup (4 ounces) shredded Mexican cheese blend
- Sour cream

1. Preheat oven to 375°F.
2. Brown beef in large skillet over medium-high heat 6 to 8 minutes, stirring to break up meat. Drain fat. Stir in tomatoes, salt, garlic powder, cumin, paprika, chili powder, ground red pepper and red pepper flakes; cook and stir 3 minutes. Stir in chips. Transfer to 13×9-inch baking dish.
3. Bake 15 to 20 minutes or until heated through. Sprinkle with green onions and cheese. Serve with sour cream.

Chicken Vindaloo

Makes 4 servings

- 1 onion, coarsely chopped
- ⅓ cup white vinegar
- 2 tablespoons tomato paste
- 1 tablespoon minced fresh ginger
- 3 cloves garlic
- 1½ teaspoons sweet paprika
- 1 teaspoon salt
- 1 teaspoon ground coriander
- 1 teaspoon ground turmeric
- ½ teaspoon dry mustard
- ½ teaspoon ground cumin
- ½ teaspoon ground red pepper
- 1½ pounds boneless skinless chicken thighs
- ¼ cup water
- 3 cups hot cooked rice
- Chopped fresh cilantro

1. Combine onion, vinegar, tomato paste, ginger, garlic, paprika, salt, coriander, turmeric, mustard, cumin and red pepper in food processor or blender; process until smooth.
2. Place chicken in large bowl. Pour spice mixture over chicken; stir to coat. Cover and marinate in refrigerator at least 1 hour or overnight.
3. Pour chicken and marinade into Dutch oven; stir in water. Bring to a boil over high heat. Reduce heat to medium low; cover and cook 20 minutes or until chicken is cooked through (165°F).
4. Transfer chicken to plate; tent with foil to keep warm. Cook sauce in Dutch oven over medium heat until sauce reduces and thickens slightly, stirring frequently. Return chicken to sauce; stir to coat. Serve chicken and sauce with rice. Top with cilantro.

Spicy Macaroni and Cheese

Makes 4 to 6 servings

- ½ cup dry milk powder
- ½ teaspoon crushed red pepper flakes
- ½ teaspoon smoked paprika
- ½ teaspoon salt
- ¼ teaspoon black pepper
- 2 cups uncooked elbow macaroni
- ½ cup sun-dried tomatoes, cut into thin strips
- ½ cup chopped crisp-cooked bacon
- 2 cups (8 ounces) shredded sharp Cheddar cheese
- 2½ cups milk
- 1 cup water
- ½ cup seasoned croutons

1. Preheat oven to 350°F. Spray 3-quart baking dish with nonstick cooking spray.
2. Combine milk powder, red pepper flakes, paprika, salt and black pepper in large bowl. Add macaroni, tomatoes and bacon bits. Stir in cheese, milk and water. Pour mixture into prepared baking dish; cover tightly with foil.
3. Bake 30 minutes. Remove from oven; uncover and stir well. Top evenly with croutons. Bake, uncovered, 30 minutes or until sauce is bubbly and macaroni is tender.

Index

Index

Index

Index

Index

Metric Conversion Chart

VOLUME MEASUREMENTS (dry)

1/8 teaspoon = 0.5 mL
1/4 teaspoon = 1 mL
1/2 teaspoon = 2 mL
3/4 teaspoon = 4 mL
1 teaspoon = 5 mL
1 tablespoon = 15 mL
2 tablespoons = 30 mL
1/4 cup = 60 mL
1/3 cup = 75 mL
1/2 cup = 125 mL
2/3 cup = 150 mL
3/4 cup = 175 mL
1 cup = 250 mL
2 cups = 1 pint = 500 mL
3 cups = 750 mL
4 cups = 1 quart = 1 L

VOLUME MEASUREMENTS (fluid)

1 fluid ounce (2 tablespoons) = 30 mL
4 fluid ounces (1/2 cup) = 125 mL
8 fluid ounces (1 cup) = 250 mL
12 fluid ounces (1 1/2 cups) = 375 mL
16 fluid ounces (2 cups) = 500 mL

WEIGHTS (mass)

1/2 ounce = 15 g
1 ounce = 30 g
3 ounces = 90 g
4 ounces = 120 g
8 ounces = 225 g
10 ounces = 285 g
12 ounces = 360 g
16 ounces = 1 pound = 450 g

DIMENSIONS

1/16 inch = 2 mm
1/8 inch = 3 mm
1/4 inch = 6 mm
1/2 inch = 1.5 cm
3/4 inch = 2 cm
1 inch = 2.5 cm

OVEN TEMPERATURES

250°F = 120°C
275°F = 140°C
300°F = 150°C
325°F = 160°C
350°F = 180°C
375°F = 190°C
400°F = 200°C
425°F = 220°C
450°F = 230°C

BAKING PAN SIZES

Utensil	Size in Inches/Quarts	Metric Volume	Size in Centimeters
Baking or Cake Pan (square or rectangular)	8×8×2	2 L	20×20×5
	9×9×2	2.5 L	23×23×5
	12×8×2	3 L	30×20×5
	13×9×2	3.5 L	33×23×5
Loaf Pan	8×4×3	1.5 L	20×10×7
	9×5×3	2 L	23×13×7
Round Layer Cake Pan	8×1½	1.2 L	20×4
	9×1½	1.5 L	23×4
Pie Plate	8×1¼	750 mL	20×3
	9×1¼	1 L	23×3
Baking Dish or Casserole	1 quart	1 L	—
	1½ quart	1.5 L	—
	2 quart	2 L	—